Sociolinguistic Aspects

of BRAZILIAN

PORTUGUESE:

R Deletion

LEONARDO REIS

AuthorHouse™
1663 Liberty Drive
Bloomington, IN 47403
www.authorhouse.com
Phone: 1-800-839-8640

Published by AuthorHouse 02/26/2015

ISBN: 978-1-4969-5766-5 (sc)
ISBN: 978-1-4969-5767-2 (e)

Library of Congress Control Number: 2015902395

Print information available on the last page.

Any people depicted in stock imagery provided by Thinkstock are models,
and such images are being used for illustrative purposes only.
Certain stock imagery © Thinkstock.

This book is printed on acid-free paper.

authorHOUSE®

TABLE OF CONTENTS

LIST OF APPENDICES

LIST OF TABLES

LIST OF FIGURES

Leonardo Reis

Sociolinguistic Aspects of Brazilian Portuguese: R Deletion

Abstract

This study discusses a case of sound variation and change in Brazilian Portuguese, in Brazil, which I claim is lexically implemented. More specifically, I address the potential variation concerning final R deletion in non-verbal words, which is a unique focus since most research addresses R deletion in verbs. I examine a case of linguistic prejudice, which contends that R deletion is only found amongst the lower classes in Brazil.

However, in the analysis of the first age group, the results provided interesting data, challenging some previous studies and supporting others. The aim of this study is to show how and when R deletion occurs in Brazilian Portuguese.

The first part shows the reason for this work, explains how and why I became interested in this topic, and gives a brief overview of the dissertation structure, including a short summary of each chapter.

The second part indicates the scope of this work, presents works carried out by others, which provide the theoretical context of this research, and finally, presents the hypothesis raised for this study.

In the third part I discuss the methodological issues and indicate how this work will be analysed. In the fourth part of this work I discuss the results and analyse the data collected, following the methodology presented in the previous chapter.

Finally, I present the conclusion, confirming and contrasting studies mentioned in the literature review, and in the latter part I offer some personal considerations on the issues and achievements of this work and suggest areas for future research.

To my parents

Acknowledgments

I would like to thank my father, Iébert, my mother Dagmar, my sister, Luciana, and my son, Kevin Reis, for their support and understanding during this distant journey in my life.

I would like to thank Ana Paula Huback, who is a lecturer in Language (Portuguese) at Columbia University, for her support; she supplied me with books, articles, and good information. I am also grateful for Barry Heselwood's invaluable help in phonetics. In addition, Monica Duchnowski deserves special thanks for her assistance in the final stages of publication.

Finally, I would like to thank my supervisor Melinda Whong for her support and kindness. She guided me through my writing and gave me crucial ideas and suggestions and without her help I would not have been able to finish my studies.

Thanks to everyone.

Chapter 1

INTRODUCTION

Portuguese is arguably a romance language spoken primarily in Portugal, Brazil, Angola, Cape Verde, Mozambique, East Timor and São Tome e Príncipe. There are approximately 200 million Portuguese speakers, which makes it the sixth most spoken language in the world.

Brazilian Portuguese is the legacy of the Portuguese colonisation of the Americas. The first Portuguese immigrants that moved to Brazil encountered other spoken languages, such as African languages and Amerindian languages used by the Jesuit missionaries (Silva Neto,1986, p. 521).

The creation of the Portuguese language stemmed from a variety of other languages, which were extremely influential in its conception, for example Latin, Spanish, Italian and French. It was through these different influences that the Portuguese language developed variations.

Both in Brazil and around the world, the variety of Portuguese used in Brazil is known as 'Brazilian Portuguese'. It is called Brazilian Portuguese perhaps due to the differences between European Portuguese and the Portuguese spoken in Brazil; it is possible to perceive differences in the accent and sometimes in the dialect, and one of the differences that have several possible variations is variable R.

The variable R exhibits many variations in Portuguese, and it is possible to have 7 variants: /X/, /ɣ/, /h/, /ɦ/, /ɾ/, /ř/ and /ř̃/. Each symbol represents a different sound of the variable R. In general, this is what is expected (Cristofaro-Silva, 2002, p. 35). See appendix 1 for a complete phonetic description of the pronunciation of R in Portuguese on page 48 (Cristofaro-Silva, 2002, pp. 38- 39).

The variable R in the first position e.g. in the word 'wiper' *rodo* in Portuguese, can be pronounced as (/X/odo), (/h/odo) or (/ř/odo); these sounds are heard in Rio de Janeiro, Belo Horizonte (the city with the third largest economy in Brazil), Lisbon, Portugal, and Sao Paulo, Brazil, respectively, the last one having its own specific dialect (Cristofaro-Silva, 2002, p. 39).

The variable R in the middle position, e.g. the word 'letter' *carta*, can be pronounced as (ca/X/ta) in Rio, (ca/h/ta) in Belo Horizonte and (ca/ɾ/ta) in Lisbon. Also, the variable R in the final position e.g. the word 'sea' *mar*, can be pronounced as (ma/X/) in Rio, (ma/h/) in Belo Horizonte and (ma/ɾ/) in Lisbon.

Basically, one can conclude from this phenomenon that in specific communicative situations, the speakers are pronouncing non-verbal words without the presence of final R in Belo Horizonte for example, in 'woman'—*mulher*, (mulhe/Ø/) instead of (mulhe/h/) and 'computer'—computador, (computado/Ø/) instead of (computado/h/).

The pronunciation of the variable R in the final position is an extremely important phenomenon to Sociolinguistics because it displays a great number of variations, which could be related to phonetic, geographical and social conditions.

This study investigated final R deletion in non-verbal words in Belo Horizonte, Brazil, and suggests a different view from (Bueno, 1944, p. 54), (Stavrou, 1947, p. 30) and (Cunha, 1968, p. 76) who concluded that this linguistic occurrence develops through illiteracy, often caused by poor education or poor social/economic backgrounds and confirmed studies by (Votre, 1978), (Oliveira, 1983, 1997) and (Huback, 2003) who disagreed with Bueno, Stravou and Cunha.

This research used the speech of 12 informants to investigate the occurrence of this phenomenon. Internal and external factors were used for the final analysis. Due to the scope of this work I investigated only non-verbal words, classifying them as substantives, adjectives and connectives (adverbs and prepositions).

Besides these factors, there are two theories of sound change, the Lexical Diffusion (LD) and Neogrammarian (NG). The Neogrammarians were a German school of linguistics who proposed the (NG) hypothesis of the regularity of sound change. According to this hypothesis, the sound change affects all words simultaneously, without exception (Bynon, 1997, p. 173).

The theory of lexical diffusion stands in contrast to the Neogrammarian hypothesis, according to which sound change applies simultaneously to all words in which its context is found. However, these two models will be discussed in chapter II.

One of the main reasons that the theme of R deletion was chosen is personal; the pronunciation of this variable has followed me since I was a child. I used to live in São Paulo, Belo Horizonte, and Florianópolis. All these cities have a different pronunciation of the variable R and after I began to study sociolinguistics during my master's degree, I saw the possibility of investigating this situation.

The lay out of this dissertation apart from chapter I is organised as follows:

- Chapter II discusses the literature review, presenting the main works carried out, and also analyses the main points of the Neogrammarian and Lexical Diffusion models.

- Chapter III shows the methodology used, with the type of data, collection methods and the methods of data analysis. This chapter also gives relevant information about the city investigated, Belo Horizonte.

- Chapter IV discusses the results and presents the analysis of the R deletion phenomenon. This chapter also discuss the internal and external factors presented throughout this work.

- Chapter V concludes this work, contrasts and confirms results discussed in the literature review, and presents reflections on this work; it also makes suggestions for future research.

Chapter 2

LITERATURE REVIEW

Research has been carried out on R deletion in verbs and non-verbal words in Brazilian Portuguese, mainly in informal speech. In this chapter I discuss the R deletion since the time when Latin and 'Old Portuguese' were spoken, French, Spanish, and Brazilian Portuguese, mainly in Belo Horizonte, Brazil.

The R deletion can also occur in English. I shall examine other people's work in order to provide a good overview of this phenomenon. It is very important to mention that even though my work is limited to the analysis of final R deletion in non-verbal words, I discuss instances of final R deletion in other situations.

There is a debate on the analysis of sound change; linguists have tried to resolve the differences between the Neogrammarian and the Diffusionist models.Due to the length of this thesis, I analysed the basic points of both models and the main findings on R deletion in the languages cited above.

2.1 – R deletion in Latin and Portuguese

History shows that R deletion occurred even before Portuguese, in Latin, the language from which Portuguese originated. The first document about this phenomenon is found in the Probi Appendix, Viennese Code, which is a phonetic list of words illustrating this phenomenon (Silva Neto, 1938, p. 9). This Probi Appendix was published in 1887; however, it was written in the 3rd century A.D., when Vulgar Latin was used.

In the Probi Appendix a total number of 227 words shows the possibility of R deletion. This is the first reference to R deletion. For example, in this list, the word *persica* is shown as being pronounced without the presence of R *pessica* (Silva Neto, 1938, p. 76).

There are other important examples of the R deletion in the work of Gil Vicente (1465-1536), in his theatre productions of the 16th Century, which demonstrate the speech of lower class communities, blacks, Jews, labourers and gypsies (Huback, 2003, p. 16) for example;

1. Beth irá se <u>casar</u> com Jack;

- Beth will if marry with Jack

- 'Beth is going to marry Jack'.

2. Eu preciso <u>falar</u> com você;

- I need speak with you;

- 'I need to speak to you'.

This situation used to occur in Portugal; the expected pronunciation and the translation of the underlined words were respectively: (caza/ɾ/), and (fala/ɾ/). However, Vicente would make his actors pronounce: (caza/Ø/) and (fala/Ø/). The idea of R deletion in this situation was to show a social class difference.

R deletion is an old phenomenon, originating in Vulgar Latin. It is also important to mention that this phenomenon is seen as a characteristic of the lower class population.

2.2 – R deletion in other languages

R deletion is not a phenomenon related only to Latin and Old Portuguese. It occurs in other romance languages, in English, which is not a romance language, and in European Portuguese and Portugal's African colonies. In the next 3 sections I analyse the occurrence of R deletion and other types of consonant deletion in these languages.

2.2.1 – R deletion in other romance languages

R deletion can be noted in two other romance languages: French and Spanish. In French, final R deletion is more frequent in conjugation of verbs after /i/, in the third conjugation of verbs after /d/ and /t/, and in the words *noir* and *soir* (Oliveira, 1983, p.76).

In Spanish, the existence of R deletion is shown in the following examples (Oliveira, 1983, p. 77):

3. El es un <u>cazador</u>;

- He is a hunter;

- 'He is a hunter'

4. Yo le vi <u>ayer</u>;

- I you saw yesterday;

- 'I saw you yesterday'.

The expected pronunciation and the translation of the underlined words are, respectively: (cazado/ɾ/) and (aye/ɾ/), however, it is possible to hear (cazado/Ø/) and (aye/Ø/). (Oliveira,1983, p.77)

2.2.2 – R deletion in English

According to Wells (1982, p. 218), R deletion may happen with the internal factor or with the following word. The following word factor is analysed in the methodology chapter; for example, in English if the next word starts with a vowel, there is no deletion. For example:

5. Her <u>car is</u> black.

The word *car* is followed by *is*, which starts with the vowel /i/ ; in this situation R in the word *car* is not deleted. The same does not occur when the following word starts with a consonant or it is in final position, for example:

6. Could you open the <u>door, please</u>?

7. You should speak to the <u>driver</u>.

In the example 6 the word *door* is followed by *please* which begins with a consonant and example 7 the word *driver* is in final position, which is considered a pause as an internal factor.

However, R deletion has no effect on initial or intervocalic R, as in red, thread, arrive, marry, in words such as fearing and barring, though it does affect feared and barred.

2.2.3 – R deletion in European Portuguese and African Portuguese-speaking countries.

In European Portuguese, the main research conducted with regards to R deletion was by Leite (1928, p.199) when he analysed the way in which R deletion in verbs is related to a pre-consonantal (R followed by a consonant) word within the informal speech of a specific coast community, for example:

8. Vou comprar leite se não <u>for</u> muito tarde;

- Will buy milk if no be very late;

- 'I will buy some milk if it is not <u>too</u> late'.

<u>The expected pronunciation is instead of (fo/ɾ/), however, it is possible to hear; (fo/Ø/), and it could be because there is a pre-consonantal word muito, 'too'.</u>

In Africa where Portuguese is spoken, and amongst the lower classes of Damão, Macau and Cabo Verde, however, the final R is generally deleted in infinitive verbs. However, according to Leite (1928 in Huback, 2003, p. 20), in Malaca, the R is usually deleted in any word with a final R, for example:

9. Tenho que <u>fazer</u> minha cama;

- Have that make my bed;

- 'I have to <u>make</u> my bed'.

10. Minha <u>mulher</u> é mandona;

- My woman is bossy;

- 'My <u>wife</u> is demanding'.

<u>The expected pronunciation is respectively: (faze/ʃ/) and (mulhe/ʃ/), however, it is possible to hear (faze/Ø/) in Damão, Macau, Cabo Verde and Malaca, and (mulhe/Ø/) in Malaca.</u>

2.2.4 – R deletion in Brazilian Portuguese

According to Juca-Filho (1937, p.112), in Brazilian Portuguese, there are many discussions on R deletion. There is a tendency for consonant deletion in the final syllable position, even though it occurs internally. For example:

11. Fevereiro tem <u>carnaval</u>;

- February have carnival;

- 'The carnival is in February'.

12. O <u>mesmo</u> por favor;

- The same per favour;

- 'The same for me please'.

<u>The expected pronunciation is, respectively: (Ka/h/naval) and (me/s/mo), however, it is possible to hear; (ka/Ø/naval) and (me/Ø/mo).</u>

In polite and more educated speech, when the word is in the middle of a sentence and is followed by a pre-consonantal word, the R is not pronounced. Stavrou (1947, p.30) and Teyssier (1990, p. 83) disagree with this statement; they mentioned that the R deletion is due to a lack of education and relates it to social class. These two analyses showed their sociolinguistic view of this phenomenon. Leite (1928, p.133) mentions that one of the main characteristics of the "Brazilian dialect" is final R deletion.

One of the main debates centers upon the influence of the Tupi, an indigenous group, the first group found in Brazilian lands before the colonisation by the Portuguese.However, this influence cannot be considered the reason for R deletion in Brazilian Portuguese, since in the Tupi language R is pronounced whenever it is present (Mello, 1981, p. 57).

Due to colonisation, slaves were brought from Africa to Brazil and were forced to build the nation. The African influence brought some phonetic alterations to Brazilian Portuguese. One of them is the R deletion (Mendonça, 1973, p.63). However, Mello (1981) disagrees with this point of view Barros-Oliveira (2001, p. 7).

2.2.4.1 – R deletion in Belo Horizonte

Marco Antônio de Oliveira (1983) and Ana Paula Huback (2003) analysed R deletion in Belo Horizonte. Oliveira obtained the following results in 1978:

- The final R is deleted more in verbs than in nouns. 81.59% in verbs and 26.09% in nouns.

- The final R is deleted more than the internal one. 70.83% final position, for example: *amor* and 17.59% internal position for example in the *word* perda.

- The final R is deleted more amongst the lower classes.

- There is no significant difference between genders.

- Teenagers (up to 20 years old) delete the final R in nouns and the older speakers in verbs.

- There is no significant difference between social classes; however, there is discrimination.

In 1997, Oliveira made a different analysis of the same phenomenon, R deletion; however, this time he adopted a diffusionist view based on the lexical diffusion model and he stated that:

> I will say that all sound changes are lexically implemented, that is, there are no neogrammarian sound changes (although we can have neogrammarian long-term end results). (Oliveira,1991, p. 103)

Huback (2003) analysed the final R deletion in nominals and produced the following results:

- R deletion is not due to a phonetic purpose, so the (NG) hypothesis was not confirmed.

- The data investigated showed that the changes occur word by word and not at the same time.

- The age group factor was not considered relevant for the sound change.

- Informants had different results according to their groups, such as: age group, social class, gender and education.

- The gender factor was also irrelevant, even though males produced more deletion than females.

- Even though there are differences in the social class factor, these differences are irrelevant for the analysis of this phenomenon.

2.3 – Sound change models

All the considerations mentioned above, except Oliveira (1997) are based on the Neogrammarian model from the concept of sound change, the main linguistic pattern since the 19th century.

In linguistic literature, one of the most interesting questions is the discussion between two different models of analysing sound change: the Neogrammarian and the Diffusionist.

2.3.1 – The Neogrammarian model

The (NG) model states that sound change is regular; that it occurs at the same time; and that the phonetic condition indicates this change. According to Bynon (1986, pp. 24-5) if the same phonetic sound changes, all the words will be affected by the change in the same way, for example:

13. Um <u>lugar</u> lindo;

- One place beautiful;

- 'A beautiful place'.

The R in the word 'place' *lugar* in Portuguese can have different sounds in Brazilian Portuguese. For example; (luga/X/) in Rio and (lugar/h/) in Belo Horizonte. However, in order to explain a second possibility of sound change in Belo Horizonte, (luga/Ø), <u>the Neogrammarian model would say that all the words with a final R would change the same way. This change is phonetic and all words within the same environment are affected by this change in the same way</u> (Wang, 1977, p.148).

Besides, in the (NG) model, the external factors such as social class, gender and age do not have any effect on the sound change. Denying those variables is the same as denying that the language is directly linked to the speakers and the communication situations they encounter. Any attempt to deny these factors results in a lack of linguistic analyses (Wang, 1977, p. 149).

The (NG) model drove linguistic studies from 1900 to 1969. Then, linguists started questioning the Neogrammarian approach, and, based on Chinese dialect data, they presented a new model, "the lexical diffusion", to explain the sound change phenomenon.

2.3.2 – The Lexical Diffusion model

The (LD) model points out that sound change is irregular; it does not occur at the same time, and the phonetic condition is not solely responsible for the change. Respecting external linguistic factors, Wang (1977, p. 151) mentioned that sound change occurs gradually, word by word and not at the same time, for example:

14. Ela não pode ir com você;

- She no can go with you;

- 'She can't go with you'.

The R in the verb 'go' ir in Portuguese can have different sounds in Brazilian Portuguese, for example; (i/X/) in Rio and (i/h/) in Belo Horizonte. However, in order to explain a second possibility of sound change in Belo Horizonte, (i/Ø/), the (LD) model explains that this change is gradual; it affects the word from time to time and it is not an abrupt change. This change occurs first in the word and then phonetically, and it does not affect all the words at the same time.

One of the main differences is what controls the change; for the NG model it is first phonetic rather than lexical. However, for the LD model, it is lexical rather than phonetic (Oliveira, 1997, p.35). Labov (1981, pp. 303-4) came to the conclusion that:

> My own position is more radical than Wang and Chen, and I will say that *all* sound changes are lexically implemented, that is, there are no Neogrammarian sound changes (although we can have neogrammarian long-term end results).

Research about lexical diffusion came last, with Betty Phillips and Joan Bybee. Both works challenged opinions on the diffusionist theory and proposed new concepts such as lexical item frequency.

Phillips (2000, p.1) argued that sound change affects some items before others and that this change is not only related to a phonetic context. So, the question is what determines that one word should be affected before other words? Phillips comments that the frequency factor was considered before Schuchardt (1885, p. 58) claimed that more frequent words would change first, and then less frequent.

> The higher the frequency of the derived form, the weaker the mapping between it and the basic form. High-frequency irregulars are resistant to regularization not because their connections with their base are better established, but because they are themselves lexically stronger. (Bybee, 1995, p. 432)

2.4 – Conclusion

After gathering all the comments cited in this literature review about R deletion in Portuguese it is possible to come to some conclusions. It is important to mention that the R deletion in the final or internal position has existed since the time when Latin was spoken, and is not restricted to the Portuguese language, whether European or Brazilian. This phenomenon also occurs in French, Spanish and English.

Analyses produced by Teyssier (1990) suggested that this situation is due to social class. However, Marroquim (1945) and Oliveira (1997) denied this social linguistic variable. They have a different perspective, in which R deletion occurs in all social classes.

However, I only investigated the final R deletion phenomenon, in non-verbal words, as mentioned in the introduction. One of my intentions is to verify whether this phenomenon belongs to a certain social class and whether there is a difference between age groups. Based on these studies and under the diffusionist focus, the hypotheses raised by this phenomenon are:

- There is R deletion in non-verbal words in Belo Horizonte;

- The variation /Ø/ does not only occur amongst lower classes;

- Final R deletion in non-verbal words in Belo Horizonte is higher within informal speech;

- R deletion is higher when the following word begins with a consonant.

## Chapter 3

METHODOLOGY

In this chapter I discuss the type of data, the data collection methods and the methods of data analysis. It is important to mention that my work was inspired by Oliveira (1983). Oliveira was supervised by William Labov, a pioneer in sociolinguistic studies, who investigated R deletion in verbs in Belo Horizonte.

However, since the data collection was taken in Belo Horizonte, Brazil, I discuss information about this city, and also about the division of social class and age group.

3.1 – Type of data

3.1.1 – Belo Horizonte – Brazil

Brazil is divided into 26 states with a population of 186 million inhabitants. Belo Horizonte, 'beautiful horizon' in English, is the capital of the State of Minas Gerais. It was founded in 1987 and it is the third largest city in Brazil after Rio de Janeiro and Sao Paulo, with a population of 2.5 million in an area of 330, 90 km. (Retrieved from Belotur website, 2006).

A map of Brazil is shown below; the red dot represents Belo Horizonte. Brazil is the only country in South America where Portuguese is spoken. All other countries speak Spanish, for example, Argentina, Chile, Colombia, and Paraguay, among others.

Figure 1. Map of Brazil. The red dot represents Belo Horizonte

Retrieved July 10, 2006, from http://www.belohorizonte.mg.gov.br/ por/a_cidade_mapa.php.

Belo Horizonte, like any other large city, has different social classes; however, we can divide them into lower class, middle class and upper class. These are general divisions, as it is arguable who actually belongs to each group.

I contacted The Brazilian Institute of Geography and Statistics (IBGE), which produces statistics, and I also contacted the department of Sociology at the Federal University of Minas Gerais, located in Belo Horizonte. Unfortunately, they did not have data regarding the division of classes or how this division is calculated, so this study will lack this information. However, the location is an important factor according to Labov (1966 in Coupland and Jaworski, 1997, p. 170).

3.2 – Internal and external factors

Linguists must analyse the internal factors, in order to check the phonetic context and morphological structure, and also the external factors such as: age, social class, which will say whether a linguistic phenomenon shows any relation to its social context; otherwise, a deeper investigation of the phenomenon will not be possible (Weinreich, Labov and Herzog, 1968, p. 176).

3.2.1 – Internal factors

The objective of the analyses of the internal factors is to observe whether R deletion has any structural relation. The internal factors selected are similar to the ones established by Huback (2003). This is to verify whether the variation or linguistic change occurs word by word. In order to analyse the function of the phonetic context in R deletion, some factors were selected for a better analysis of this phenomenon.

3.2.1.1 – Following word

The following word factor represents the importance of the next word in the R deletion phenomenon, for example:

15. Vowel

- O vendedor é excelente;

- The salesman is excellent;

- 'The salesman is excellent',

16. Consonant

- O jogador saiu do jogo mais cedo;

- The player left of game more early;

- 'The player left the game earlier'.

17. Pause

- Pergunta para o <u>doutor;</u>

- Ask for the doctor;

- 'Ask the doctor'.

This factor was selected because some analyses in other phonological processes considered the following segment as facilitator for the deletion. In example 15, the word *vendedor* appears before the vowel /e/; consequently, the following word could change the pronunciation of R in the word *vendedor*. A possible occurrence is the formation of a new syllable, as these two elements could merge. It was expected that the informant would merge *vendedor* with é, forming *vendedore*.

In example 16, the word *jogador* appears before a consonant; consequently, the following word could change the pronunciation of R, however, in contrast with the previous example, it was expected that the informant would delete the R in the word *jogador*. In English, if the following word starts with a consonant, the occurrence of deletion of t/*d* is higher than with a following vowel, Labov (1972, p. 217).

In the last example, the following word is called a 'pause'; the final full stop after doutor pauses the sentence. This pause could also change the pronunciation of the final R.

3.2.1.2 – Number of syllables

The number of syllables factor represents the importance of the quantity of syllables in the R deletion phenomenon, for example:

- Monosyllable – (pair/par, flour/flor)

- Polysyllable – (player/jogador, director/diretor)

The number of syllables factor was selected because the fact that a word is monosyllabic or polysyllabic can cause R deletion (Amaral, 1976, p. 52).However, I considered a polysyllabic word to be any word with two or more syllables. Studies confirmed that there is not a significant difference between disyllabic and polysyllabic words in this respect (Oliveira, 1981, p. 35).

I investigated the monosyllabic and polysyllabic words and confirmed that the deletion is lower when the word is monosyllabic.

3.2.1.3 – Non-verbal words

The non-verbal word factor represents the word class in the R deletion phenomenon; I divided them as, for example:

- Substantive (computer/computador)

- Adjective (bigger/maior)

- Connectives (prepositions and adverbs), prepositions (by/por), and adverbs (slower/ devagar)

The non-verbal word factor was selected because with this data I investigated whether the deletion affects all words at the same time or whether it starts with a particular one. Results showed a higher rate of deletion in substantives (Oliveira, 1997, p. 34).

All the internal factors considered together make it possible to see whether this phenomenon occurs in all words at the same time, as in the Neogrammarian approach, or whether it happens gradually, word by word, as in the lexical diffusion approach.

3.2.2 – External factors

The objective of the external factors is to investigate whether this phenomenon is related to social factors, and which speakers delete the variable R and on which occasion. The external factors analysed were age group, social class and style.

Language is an institution with an autonomy of its own, one must therefore determine the general conditions of development from a purely linguistic point of view; . . . but since language is [also] a social institution, it follows that linguistics is a social science, and the only variable element to which one may appeal in order to account for a linguistic change is social change, of which language variations are but the consequences – sometimes immediate and direct, and more often mediated and indirect. (Meillet, 1906a, p.17; Weinreich, Labov and Herzog, 1968, p. 176)

3.2.2.1 – Age Group

The age group factor was selected in order to investigate whether there is a linguistic change in progress. According to the theory of variation, a language is learned when the person is young, after this phase the speaker does not change much of his or her speech (Chambers, 1995, pp. 184-5).

Based on this study, it is possible to affirm that today, in 2015, an informant who is (46) or older (60) has the same speech as when he or she was (15-20) years old, from 1940 to 1960. Accordingly, it is relevant to this analysis to check whether there is a modification over time.

This type of methodology is essential, since we cannot investigate this situation in real time. All the informants were born in the city of Belo Horizonte. The 3 age groups selected were: A—(15-25) years old, B—(26-45) and C—(46-60).

3.2.2.2 – Social class

Social class is still not defined by sociologists. This term has been studied for a long time. Karl Marx tried to define it more specifically; however, his masterpiece *Capital* was not finished. His next step in this direction would have been the concept of social class (Santos, in Huback, 2003, p. 84).

Since it is difficult to define social class, I took into consideration the following points: occupation, education, income and residential area. However, in Belo Horizonte, it is generally assumed that people who reside and are homeowners in the area around Lake Pampulha and south of the city center are middle class. In order to qualify as middle class, they should have at least an undergraduate diploma and an income of U$35,000 per year. I considered informants living in other areas, without a diploma, and with an income of less than U$5,000 per year, to be lower class.

> The social status of an individual is determined by the subjective reactions of other members of society, but it is easier for outsiders to use objective social and economic indicators to approximate the position of given individuals. In the United States, we obtain the sharpest overall stratification with various combinations of occupation, education, income and residential area. In studying historical records, we usually judge upper-class figures by their family connections and title; less prominent individuals are easiest to classify by their occupations and habitual associations. (Labov,1972, p. 285)

The social class factor was selected due to the reasons mentioned in the literature review. The upper class was excluded due to the difficulty of arranging interviews. The social classes analysed are: lower class and middle class. See appendix (3 on page 50) for informant classification sheet.

3.3 – Styles of interview

The style is one of the factors that determine how the speakers use the language. The more formal the style is, the higher is the occurrence of the standard form, and the less formal, the less the standard form is spoken. The more attention is paid to speech, and the more formal the speech is, the less attention the speaker pays to his or her speech, and the less formality is expected (Labov, 1973, p. 9). These styles were considered for this work:

- Informal interview;

- Text reading in which there are ocurrences of the final R in non-verbal words; (see appendix 4, page 51)

- Word list reading in which there are ocurrences of the Final R in non-verbal words; (see appendix 5, page 52)

In the informal interview, formal speech was expected at the beginning of the interview, and moments of lesser formality were expected when informants were talking about their life and dreams. Labov suggested in his studies in New York to ask "danger of death" questions to the informants in order to make them act as naturally as possible. Labov suggested that if the informants are under emotion then natural speech would occur. After the informal interview the informants read a text and a list of words. It was expected that informants would maintain the use of the final R during the word list and text reading parts of the interview since there is no single style of speakers (Labov, 1973, p. 9).

I mixed words with a final R among others. Since this is a list of words, the informants paid more attention reading this than during the informal interview. In the word list the word factor used was 'pause'. Pause was selected because the words are not in a text or a sentence format.

3.4 – Data Collection Methods

Twelve people were divided into three groups of four informants: A, B and C; and, as mentioned before, every group included two lower class informants and two middle class informants, making a total of twelve who were interviewed.

My father, who is an engineer, contacted the middle class informants, all friends; Edgar, who is (62) years old and his daughter Yasline (30), Celia (41) and her daughter Cristiane (24), Bruno (23) and Lucia (60) and my sister contacted the lower class informants; Nautilus (54), Estaurina (46), Junior (29), Marcio (28), Douglas (22) and Denis (21), Luciana, my sister, works as a food engineer, she makes inspections in restaurants, bars and caterings and she is always in contact with the general public.

3.4.1 – Conducting the interview

The interviews had to follow a strict pattern in order to get the data. Interviews should last up to two hours for each speaker (Labov, in Milroy, 1997, p. 39). According to Milroy, it is difficult to say what the exact length of the interview should be, considering that phonological data can be obtained from an interview of 20 to 30 minutes (Milroy, 1997, p. 39). Due to the scope of this work, interviews took no longer than ten minutes for each informant.

A tape-recorder was used to collect the data. William Labov, a pioneer in sociolinguistic research, used the term 'Observer's Paradox' with reference to the most natural way to collect spoken data, from casual speech (Labov, 1972, p. 209) ; at the same time the researcher is obtaining his or her data, his or her presence might affect people's behavior (Cameron, 2001, p. 20).

One of the ways of producing informal speech is to ask the informants a "danger of death" question. The informant is placed in an emotional situation, which produces informal speech (Labov, in Milroy, 1997, p. 40). Data should be colleted in a real life situation, for example when students are leaving university or saying goodbye to classmates (Coupland and Jaworski,1997, p. 69).

The tape recorder was not hidden; since according to Cameron (2001, p.22), informants should know in advance when spoken data is being collected to avoid future complications, such as refusing permission for their voice to be used for research, or reasons of privacy or of feeling betrayed. Honesty at this stage is the best way to deal with this situation. See appendix (2 on page 49) for informants' authorization sheet.

For the interview I wrote out questions to be inserted during the conversation where the occurrence of a final R in a non-verbal word would occur. The interview was based on questions related to their way of life in the city, how Belo Horizonte changed with time, what they did for fun, questions about their youth for the old ones, peoples' attitudes, "danger of death" questions and questions about their aspirations in life.

In the beginning of the interview they were tense; however, later, they actually forgot the tape recorder was there and spoke more naturally, which confirms Milroy's studies.

The lower class interviews were more difficult to conduct. They had to be done in public places and sometimes noises would interfere; one of the interviews had to be cancelled due to the noise in the background. After the interview, informants were asked to read the text and the list of words.

3.4.2 – Transcribing the data

In the transcription phase I listened to all the tapes, to see whether they were of sufficient quality to determine whether there was an R deletion situation. When transcribing the informal interview, I wrote all non-verbal words with a final R; with the text and the list of words, I made one copy of the passage and list for each informant, and I listened, ticking when final R deletion occurred. See appendix (6 to 6.12 pages 53 to 65) for complete informant transcription.

In the informal interview I wrote down all non-verbal words spoken by each informant and circled the ones with final R deletion. At the end of my transcription I had a list of non-verbal words and non-verbal words with final R deleted for each informant with the total of 683 words and 83 with a final R deleted.

3.5 – Methods of data analysis

In order to analyse all the collected data I had to create a codification key and make a word-by-word codification, so I could teach the VARBRUL programme, which is linguistic software for variable research, to process the data and give me percentages and probabilities. This is the same program used for the research undertaken by Oliveira, mentioned throughout this research. Retrieved July 25, 2006, from Goldvarb website http://www.york.ac.uk/ depts/lang/ webstuff/goldvarb.

I created a code for internal and external factors, and for each informant, the codes are as follows:

1. R deletion; **D**—Delete and **N**—Non-delete

2. Number of syllables; **M**—Monosyllable and **P**—Polysyllable

3. Following word; **V**—Vowel, **C**—Consonant and **P**—Pause

4. Word class; **S**—Substantive, **A** – Adjective and **C** – Connectives (Prepositions and adverbs)

5. Style; **I** –Informal, **T** –Text and **L** – Word list

6. Social class; **L** –Lower Class and **M** – Middle class

7. Age Group; **A** – 15-25, **B** – 26-45 and **C** – 46-60

8. Informants; **Y** for Denis, **W** –Douglas, **R** –Junior, **S** –Marcio, **H** –Nautilus, **F** –Estaurina, **G** –Edgar, **P** –Lucia, **Z** –Bruno, **K** –Cristiane, **X** –Celia and **V** for Yasline.

The next step was to codify all 683 words collected in the interview; for example, the word 'bigger' (maio*r) in* Portuguese, was codified according to the informant, such as the informant 'Junior' (R), 29 years old, age group B and L (lower class). In order to codify the word I had to respect the order I had created when teaching the program the codification key. This program only reads codes not words, so they must be created in advance; otherwise, VARBRUL does not understand any input.

This program only accepts codes starting with a parenthesis; for example, the word maio*r according* to informant R had the following codification:

- **(DPCAILBR MAIOX—1 ***

There must not be any space between the letters and between the parenthesis and the first code. In this real example (see appendix for complete word and key codification), the first code is (D) for deleted, which means that the informant (R) deleted the final R, the code (P) is for polysyllabic word, (C) means that the following word is a consonant, (A) because the word *maior* is an adjective, (I) because it was in an informal style, (L) indicates that the informant belongs to the lower class, (B) indicates the informant's age group (25-45), and (R) represents the informant. The program cannot read anything after only one space; therefore, I pressed the space bar twice to be safe, and after that, I added information for my control. I wrote the word, if the R was deleted I put an X instead of R, and finally I added a number to help me count the words. (*) This symbol is also a reminder of the final R deletion. See appendix (7 to 7.12, pages 66 to 78) for complete codification Key and word codification for each informant.

Chapter 4

DATA ANALYSIS

I analysed the 683 data collected, and all the data was submitted to the VARBRUL program, for statistical analysis. It is important firstly to have a full view of the results. At the end of this chapter, I discuss all factors suggested in the methodology. The internal and external factors which the program considered relevant for the analysis are:

- Age group.

- Social class.

- Styles.

- Informants.

- The following word.

- Number of syllables.

- Non-verbal words.

4.1 – Total data results

Before the analysis of each factor, this is the final result for the final R deletion in non-verbal words in Belo Horizonte. Table 1 shows the total words with the presence of final R and R deletion:

Data	%
81/683	11.8

Table 1: Total statistic of R deletion (683 words with final R).

The total result showed the occurrence of 683 words with final R; however, the 12 informants deleted the final R in 81 words, that is, 11.85% of the total.

Due to the number of informants (12) and due to the scope of this dissertation it was not possible to have more data for a larger analysis. However, the percentage of 11.85% indicates that this phenomenon exists in Belo Horizonte and we shall investigate which factors contribute to this R deletion and how this deletion is sociolinguistically divided.

4.2 – General table analysis

This table provides general information on each informant. The first column on the left refers to the informants from bottom to top. The first four informants belong to age group A—(15-25), then B—(26-45), and finally C – (46-60). The lower class informants are shaded.

The second column represents the first style used, the informal interview. The third, fifth, seventh and ninth columns show percentages of R deletion. The fourth column represents the text style, and the sixth column, the word list style. The eighth column contains the total of words for each informant.

Finally, the probability column represents a measure of how likely this event is to occur. Probability is usually measured between 0 and 1 where 0 indicates that the event has no likelihood of the event occurring (0%) and 1 where the event is infinitely guaranteed to happen (100%). Throughout this analysis I will, however, be representing probability by percentage as well as by the standard format. The probability will be discussed in the last section of this chapter.

All the styles are present in columns (number of R deleted / number of words spoken with a final R). Since the informant G did not delete the final R in any occasion, it is shown to be likely that this informant will be among the least likely to delete the R. However, it is impossible to say that informant G will maintain a 0% probability of this fact in the longer term with such a small sample size. An analysis follows table 2.

Age groups	Informants	Informal interview	%	Text	%	Word list	%	Total	%	Probability	
C	G	0/10	0	0/26	0	0/19	0	0/55	0	x	x
	P	1/10	10	0/26	0	0/19	0	1/55	1.8	0,153	15.3%
	H	6/12	50	2/26	7.6	1/19	5.2	9/57	15.7	0,673	67.3%
	F	4/12	33.3	1/26	3.8	0/19	0	5/57	8.7	0,490	49.0%
B	V	1/11	9.0	0/26	0	0/19	0	1/56	1.78	0,115	11.5%
	X	1/12	8.3	0/26	0	0/19	0	1/57	1.75	0,128	12.8%
	S	8/12	66.6	2/26	7.6	0/19	0	10/57	17.5	0,682	68.2%
	R	5/11	45.4	6/26	23.0	0/19	0	11/56	19.6	0,753	75.3%
A	K	5/14	35.7	0/26	0	0/19	0	5/59	8.4	0,401	40.1%
	Z	7/11	63.6	5/26	19.2	0/19	0	12/56	21.4	0,761	76.1%
	Y	7/16	43.7	8/26	30.7	1/19	5.2	16/61	26.2	0,786	78.6%
	W	5/12	41.6	5/26	19.2	0/19	0	10/57	17.5	0,715	71.5%
	Total 12	50/143	34.9	29/312	9.2	2/228	0.8	81/683	11.8	x	

Table 2: The results for informants (683 tokens/words with a final R).

Table 2 shows that R deletion occurs gradually, according to the style of interview. The more formal the speech, the less R deletion occurs. This phenomenon was mentioned in the section on style in the methodology chapter when Labov (1973, p. 9) suggested that informants must be in an informal situation in order to produce natural speech. None of the informants shows the opposite, however; informant G did not delete the R on any occasion.

Another point demonstrated by table 2 is that lower class informants have a higher number of deletions than the middle classes. Although age group A shows the opposite, if we add both percentages together, 8.53% for the lower class and 9.93% for the middle class, this interesting result shows that R deletion does not only occur in the lower classes and age group A. The middle classes have a higher percentage of deletion than the lower class age group A, contrasting with studies by Teyssier (1990) cited in the literature review.

4.2.1 – Analysis of external factors

Since the external factors produced interesting results, I analysed these first. The external factors analysed were: social class and age group. I have previously mentioned 'styles' and confirmed Labov's theory; where he suggested that in informal speech informants would show the natural language used, I, however, now discuss this factor in a more detailed analysis.

4.2.1.1 – Age group

The age group factor yielded an interesting result; figure 3 below shows the results for each age group. Age group A has the highest percentage of R deletion and age group C the lowest.

Based on the table below, we could suggest that R deletion in non-verbal words in Belo Horizonte is higher amongst young adults and lower amongst the old inhabitants of Belo Horizonte, and group B presents a balance between both, and we are also able to contrast (Chambers, 1995, pp. 184-5). When he mentioned that a language is learned when the person is young, after this phase the speaker does not change much of his or her speech.

Age Group	Data	%	Probability	
A—(15-25)	43/233	18.45	0,645	64.5%
B—(26-45)	23/226	10.17	0,445	44.5%
C – (46-60)	15/224	6.69	0,370	37.0%

Table 3: The results for age groups (683 tokens).

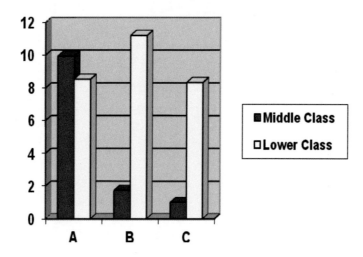

Figure 2. Age group percentage chart.

4.2.1.2 –Social Class

At first the social class factor did not produce any new results; however, we are able to compare this with the findings of Teyssier (1990) among others cited in the literature review, who claimed that R deletion is a lower class phenomenon. See table and chart for complete data.

Social Class	Data	%	Probability	
Middle class	20/318	6.28	0,316	31.6%
Lower Class	61/345	17.68	0,654	65.4%

Table 4. The results for social class.

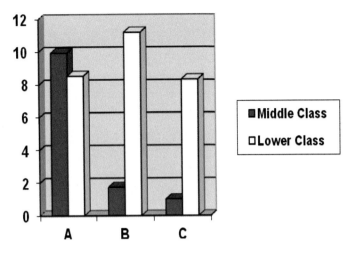

Figure 3. Social class percentage chart.

4.2.1.2.1 –Social class x age groups

The most interesting point of the external factors was when social class and age groups were crossed; however, this was only done for the informal interview. There was an average of 12 tokens per informant. This low number of tokens is due to the numbers of informants used in this research and the fact that the occurrence of non-verbal words with final R is limited.

After crossing social classes and age groups, age group A shows the most significant point produced by this analysis; the rate of R deletion amongst the middle classes is significantly higher than amongst the lower classes, in strong contrast to the findings of Teyssier (1990) among others cited in the literature review, who claimed that R deletion is a lower class phenomenon. At this stage it is important to reiterate that all middle class informants hold an undergraduate degree and live in a prestigious area in Belo Horizonte.

Figure 3 shows the modification of R deletion among age groups for the informal interview only; in the lower class results, for example, the percentage of deletion increased from age group A to age group B and then there is a decrease of deletion in age group C. However, in the middle class group, the percentage of deletion from age group A decreased considerably in relation to group B and gradually in relation to group C.

Informal Interview	Data	%
A—Middle Class	12/25	48
A—Lower Class	12/28	42.8

Table 5. Age group A

Informal Interview	Data	%
B—Middle Class	2/23	8.6
B—Lower Class	13/23	56.5

Table 6. Age group B

Informal Interview	Data	%
C—Middle Class	1/20	5
C—Lower Class	10/24	41.6

Table 7. Age group C

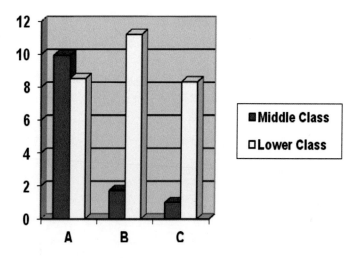

Figure 4. Social class x age groups (informal interview).
A (15-25), B (26-45) and C (46-60) age groups.

4.3 – Styles

As I mentioned in the methodology, it was expected that informants would delete the final R at a higher rate in the informal interview; even though at the beginning of the interview they were apprehensive, later, they would forget they were being interviewed and would speak normally.

As I discussed at the beginning of this chapter, there is a decreased occurrence of R deletion in the informal interview compared to the other two styles. Both social classes presented a decrease of R deletion according to style. These results confirmed Labov's theory discussed in the methodology of this study. These are the final styles results:

Styles	Data	%	Probability	
Informal	50/143	34.96	0,855	85.5%
Text	29/312	9.29	0,490	49.0%
Word list	2/228	0.87	0,248	24.8%

Table 8: The results for style (683 tokens).

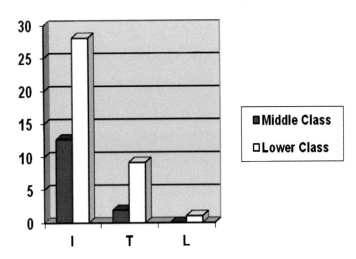

Figure 5. I (Informal interview), T (Text) and L (List of words).

4.3.1 – Informal Interview

In the informal interview we had an average of 12 tokens per informant. This low number of tokens is due to the numbers of informants used in this research and due to the fact that the occurrence of non-verbal words with final R is limited. (See appendix 5. to 5.12. for a complete view of the informal interview transcription).

This style had the highest probability of R deletion; it shows that when the speaker is acting naturally there is a tendency towards R deletion. Even though they were in the presence of a tape-recorder they deleted the final R. The following table shows the probability and total percentages for the informal interview. Since informant G did not use any deletion, he was excluded from the probability data.

Informants	Informal interview	%	Probability	
G	0/10	0	x	x
P	1/12	8.33	0,250	25.0%
H	6/12	50	0,658	65.8%
F	4/12	33.33	0,561	56.1%
V	1/11	9.09	0,154	15.4%
X	1/12	8.33	0,172	17.2%
S	8/12	66.66	0,805	80.5%
R	5/11	45.45	0,655	65.5%
K	5/14	35.71	0,397	39.7%
Z	7/11	63.63	0,748	74.8%
Y	7/16	43.75	0,484	48.4%
W	5/12	41.66	0,617	61.7%

Table 9. Informal interview.

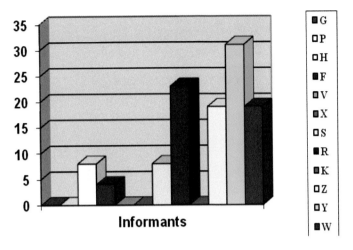

Figure 6. Informal interview chart.

4.3.2 – Text – Formal Interview

The text part of the interview had a total of 312 tokens, however, there were 29 words with R deletion. The text had 26 non-verbal words with a final R. Due to the low number of R deletions the program did not select probability as relevant.

w	Text	%
G	0/26	0
P	0/26	0
H	2/26	7.6
F	1/26	3.8
V	0/26	0
X	0/26	0
S	2/26	7.6
R	6/26	23.0
K	0/26	0
Z	5/26	19.2

Y	8/26	30.7
W	5/26	19.2

Table 10. Text interview.

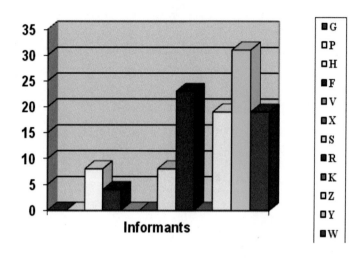

Figure 7. Text percentage chart.

4.3.3 – List of words – Formal Interview

In the list words part of the interview, there were 228 words with a final R; however, the deletion occured only twice. Informants Y and H both deleted the final R in the word *martir.* (See appendix 5.1 and 5.5 for complete interview transcription.) Due to the low rate of R deletion the program did not select probability as relevant.

Informants	Word list	%
G	0/19	0
P	0/19	0
H	1/19	5.2
F	0/19	0

V	0/19	0
X	0/19	0
S	0/19	0
R	0/19	0
K	0/19	0
Z	0/19	0
Y	1/19	5.2
W	0/19	0

Table 11. Word list interview.

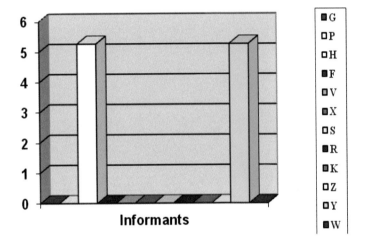

Figure 8. Word list percentage chart.

4.4 – Informants

In the informants factor, the table was divided in four columns, the first: informants, the second: complete data, the third: percentage and the fourth: probability. Informant G had to be left out of the probability column because the VARBRUL progam cannot calculate a probability if there is a 'knockout'. A 'knockout' is when one of the results is 'Zero'. The percentage is taken from the total of tokens which is 683. Informant Y was the one who deleted the final R most often. However, W, Z, and R also had a high probability number. It is important to mention that what these informants have in common is the fact that they belong to the lower class. View table and chart below:

Informants	Data	%	Probability	
G	0/55	0	x	x
P	1/55	1.8	0,153	15.3%
H	9/57	15.7	0,673	67.3%
F	5/57	8.7	0,490	49.0%
V	1/56	1.7	0,115	11.5%
X	1/57	1.7	0,128	12.8%
S	10/57	17.5	0,682	68.2%
R	11/56	19.6	0,753	75.3%
K	5/59	8.4	0,401	40.1%
Z	12/56	21.4	0,761	76.1%
Y	16/61	26.2	0,786	78.6%
W	10/57	17.5	0,715	71.5%
Total 12	81/683	11.8		

Table 12.Informants

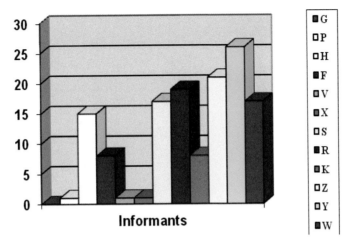

Figure 9. Informants percentage chart.
Follow the sequence from (G) left to (W) right.

4.5 – Internal factors

After the external factors analyses, I analysed the influence of the internal factors in the final R deletion in non-verbal words in Belo Horizonte. The importance of this is to investigate the structure and the function of the phonetic context in R deletion; the factors selected were: the following word, the number of syllables, and non-verbal words (Substantive, Adjectives, and Connectives).

4.5.1 – Following word

From my hypothesis, a higher R deletion was expected when the following word began with a vowel, creating new syllables, for example, *cor azul* 'blue colour'. Instead of pronouncing (co/h/ azul), it is possible to hear (co/ř/azul); however, this situation was not confirmed in this work. In English, the deletion of t/*d* is higher when followed by a vowel (Labov, 1972, p. 217).

The probabilty for the vowel and consonant are very close, which indicates that any following segment does affect the R deletion. In contrast, the pause did not produce any relevant information. It is important to remember that most 'pause' words came from the list of words data. View table and chart below:

Following word	Data	%	Probability	
Vowel	28/128	21.8	0,725	72.5%
Consonant	48/239	20.0	0,641	64.1%
Pause	5/316	1.5	0,302	30.2%

Table 13: The results for the following word (683 tokens).

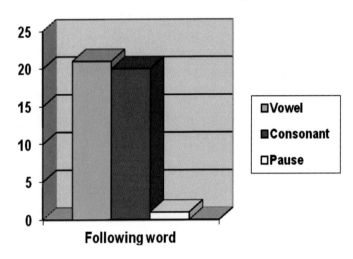

Figure 10. Following word percentage chart.

4.5.2 – Number of syllables

The number of syllables factor was selected because the fact that the word is monosyllabic or polysyllabic can cause R deletion (Amaral, 1976, p. 52). However, in dissyllables there is not a significant difference (Oliveira, 1981, p. 35). The R deletion in monosyllbic words is almost zero and we can affirm that the structural factor is relevant, as Amaral (1976, p. 52) had affirmed in his work; the deletion in monosyllabic words is practically non existant. The results are presented in the table and chart below:

Number of Syllables	Data	%	Probability	
Monosyllable	2/128	1.56	0,108	10.8%
Polysyllable	79/555	14.2	0,619	61.9%

Table 14: The results for the number of syllables (683 tokens)

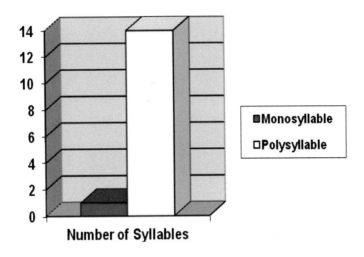

Figure 11. Number of syllables percentage chart.

4.5.3 – Non-verbal words

The non-verbal word factor was selected because with this data I investigated whether the deletion affects all words at the same time or whether it starts with a particular one (Oliveira, 1997, p. 34).

All the internal factors considered in the analyses of R deletion make it possible to see whether this phenomenon occurs in all words at the same time, as in the Neogrammarian approach, or whether it happens gradually, word by word, as in the Lexical Diffusion approach.

Non-verbal words	Data	%	Probability	
Substantives	66/520	12.6	0,453	45.3%
Adjectives	13/109	11.9	0,421	42.1%

Connectives	2/54	3.7	0,112	11.2%

Table 15: The results for the non-verbal words (683 tokens).

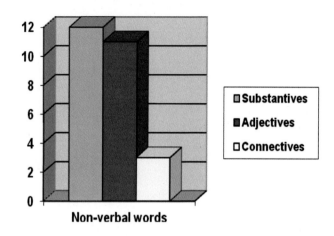

Figure 22. Non-verbal words percentage chart.

4.6 – Probability discussion of the findings

The probability as I said in the beginning of this chapter represents a measure of how likely this event tends to occur. Probability is measured between 0 and 1 where 0 indicates that the event has no likelihood of happening (0%) and 1 where the event is guaranteed to happen (100%).

There are many forms to analyse and interpret probability. The program VARBRUL presented probability when it was relevant to present. That is why in some parts of the data analysis the probability column did not appear.

We could make some considerations about the manner in which the probability is calculated according to the numbers given. As I mentioned before the probability was also given in percentage for a better understanding.

In the Age group, the probability showed for group (A) 0,645 for R deletion to happen. That means, people in Belo Horizonte from 15 to 25 years old, according to this study, have a probability of 64.5% to delete the final R in non-verbal words. The result for group (B) 0,445 is and group (C) 0,370. In order to find the percentage, you have to move the comma two digits to the right and cancel the zero before the comma.

For the Social group, the probability indicated that the middle class has 0,316 of chance to delete the final R whereas the lower class 0,654. That means, in speech the lower class has a higher possibility of deleting the R than the middle class; however, the middle class also deletes the final R.

For the Styles, the informal interview with 0,855 is far ahead with more chances to have R deletion than when someone who is reading a text with 0,490 and when someone is reading a list of words with 0,248.

If the following word starts with a vowel, the probability of R deletion is 0,725; however, if a Final R is preceded by a consonant the probability is 0,641, and if it is a final word the probability is 0,302. This result contrasted my hypothesis in chapter 2, on page 13. I expected the same results as Wells, discussed on page 6.

In the number of syllables factor, if the word is monosyllable we have 0,108 and if the word is polysyllable the probability is 0,619. We could assume that the more syllables the word has the higher is the possibility of deletion in Belo Horizonte.

Another factor, which is relevant to discuss, is the non-verbal words division, within the substantives, with 0,453, adjectives with 0,421 and connectives with 0,112. The balance shown regarding the substantives and the adjectives did not produce a significant result; however, we could interpret that there is little difference whenever the word is an adjective or substantive for the case of R deletion in Belo Horizonte.

In this section, I would like to recall the hypothesis raised at the end of chapter 2. I confirm the existence of R deletion in non-verbal words in Belo Horizonte; I also reaffirm that this R deletion is not a characteristic of lower classes, and I also confirm that the R deletion is higher within the informal speech. The only expectation denied was the following word factor. In the next chapter I state my final conclusion of this case study of R deletion in Belo Horizonte, Brazil.

Chapter 5

CONCLUSION

This study analysed final R deletion in non-verbal words in the city of Belo Horizonte, Brazil, based on the Lexical Diffusion theory. After the data collection and analysis, using internal and external factors and the styles, which were used to conduct the interviews, it is possible to reach some conclusions:

- Results confirmed previous studies; there was a total percentage of 11% final R deletion in non-verbal words in Belo Horizonte.

- R deletion in non-verbal words in Belo Horizonte is higher amongst young adults and lower amongst the older inhabitants of Belo Horizonte. Confirms Oliveira (1983).

- The social class results produced interesting data, on the whole, the lower class delete the final R in non-verbal words much more than the middle class; however, middle class informants also delete the final R as Oliveira (1983) confirms.

- The middle class informants from age group A had a higher case of R deletion than the lower class from age group A, although only in the informal interview. This result contradicts Oliveira (1983), Marroquim (1945), Stavrou (1947) and Teyssier (1990).

- As for the style of interview conducted, it was possible to confirm previous studies where the level of R deletion is higher in the informal interview compared to the other two styles. This result confirms that of Labov (1973).

- The following word factor presented an interesting point. The deletion of the final R when the next word begins with a consonant is around 1% higher than the words which start with a vowel. What was expected was a higher rate of R deletion, and a lower rate of R deletion if the next segment started with a vowel.

- R deletion in monosyllbic words is almost zero; this result showed that a structural factor can contribute to such deletion, confirming previous studies.

- R deletion is not related to any specific phonetic context. The Neogrammarian theory, which holds that a phonetic context is needed to bring about such change, was not confirmed by this specific phenomenon.

- According to the Lexical Diffusion theory, all words are not affected at the same time due to this sound change; the connectives were significantly different from the substantives and adjectives, confirming that this sound change is gradual.

This study presented some issues, which I intend to change for future research. The first and main one is the fact that I could not conduct the interviews myself. Even though my father and sister performed the task very well, if I had been there I would have been able to learn from this experience and would have tried to collect a higher number of data in the informal interview.

When I contrasted the informal interview with the passage used and the word list, it was good to confirm that the more natural the informant is, the higher the probability of R deletion. However, in a future study, I intend to conduct a deeper investigation in the informal interview, and collect data from more informants. I would also like to change the approach used in the informal interview. For future studies, I would like to try to hide the tape recorder and see if it is possible to collect more natural data, maybe by choosing one specific place for the data collection and trying to transcribe the data, even though it takes a long time.

I also think it is important to investigate if the frequency of the words would interfere in the R deletion phenomenon. Due to the scope of this study this factor could not be studied.

Another weakness was the fact that I could not find a social class division to follow. Although I have tried, this information was crucial for this study; therefore, I asked the informants to complete a form stating address, education, and income.

The program VARBRUL selected for the statistic analysis gave me good results throughout this study; however, in certain occasions it did not give me probabilities due to the low number of data.

The main challenge of this study was to deny the fact that R deletion is a characteristic of the lower class. The first age group (A) gave me one interesting result, which was the fact that the middle class informants had a higher deletion rate than the lower class.

I hope with this study on the phenomenon of R deletion in non-verbal words in the city of Belo Horizonte, Brazil, using the diffusionist theory, I have contributed to linguistics research with some information about R deletion.

References

Amaral, Amadeu. (1976). *O dialeto caipira* (3rd ed.). São Paulo: HUCITEC/Secretaria da Cultura, Ciência e Tecnologia.

Barros-Oliveira, Mariluci. (2001). Manutenção e apagamento do R final de vocábulo na fala de Itaituba (Doctoral dissertation). Universidade Federal do Pará, Belém.

Belotur. (2006). Retrieved July 25, 2006, from http://www.belohorizonte.mg.gov.br/por/a_cidade_mapa.php

Bueno, F. S. (1944). *Gramática normativa da língua portuguesa*. São Paulo: Livraria Acadêmica.

Bybee, Joan. (1995). Regular morphology and the lexicon. *Language and Cognitive Processes, 10* (5), 425-455.

Bybee, Joan. (2001). *Phonology and language use*. Cambridge: Cambridge University Press.

Bynon, Theodora. (1977). *Historical linguistics*. Cambridge: Cambridge University Press.

Bynon, Theodora. (1986). *Historical linguistics*. London: Cambridge University Press.

Cameron, D. (2001). *Working with spoken discourse*. London: Sage Publications Ltd.

Chambers, J. K. (1995). *Sociolinguistic theory: linguistic variation and its social significance*. Oxford: Blackwell.

Chen, Matthew Y. & William S-Y. Wang. (1975). Sound change: actuation and implementation. *Language, 51* (2), 255–281.

Coupland, N. & Jaworski, A. (1997). *Sociolinguistics: A reader and coursebook*. Hampshire: Macmillian.

Cristófaro-Silva, Thaïs. (2002). *Fonética e fonologia do Português*: roteiro de estudos e guia de exercícios. São Paulo: Contexto.

Cunha, Celso. (1968). *Língua portuguesa e realidade brasileira* (3rd ed.). Rio de Janeiro: Tempo Brasileiro.

Goldvarb. (2001). Retrieved August 9, 2006, from http://www.york.ac.uk/depts/lang/webstuff/goldvarb

Huback, Ana. (2003). *Cancelamento final do R em nominais. Uma abordagem diffusionista.* Belo Horizonte: UFMG.

Joseph, B.D. & Janda, R. D. (Eds.). (2003). *The handbook of historical linguistics.* Berlin: Blackwell.

Juca-Filho, C. (1937). *Língua nacional.* Rio de Janeiro: Gráfica Apollo.

Labov, William. (1966). The social stratification of (r) in New York City department stores. In N. Coupland & A. Jaworski (Eds.), *Sociolinguistics: a reader and coursebook* (pp. 168-177). Hampshire: Macmillian.

Labov, William. (1972). *Sociolinguistic patterns.* Philadelphia: University of Pennsylvania Press.

Labov, William. (1981). Resolving the neogrammarian controversy. *Language, 57* (2), 267-308.

Labov, William. (1994). A proposed resolution of the regularity question. In *Principles of linguistic change.* Oxford: Blackwell.

Labov, William. (2001). *Principles of linguistic change (Vol. 2: Social factors).* Oxford: Blackwell.

Labov, William. (1972). Language in the inner city: studies in the black English vernacular. Philadelphia: University of Pennsylvania Press.

Leite, Jose. (1928). *Opúsculos*: dialetologia. Coimbra: Imprensa da Universidade.

Marroquim, Mário. (1945). *A língua do Nordeste:* Alagoas e Pernambuco. São Paulo: Companhia Editora Nacional.

Mello, Gladstone. (1981). *A língua do Brasil* (4. ed.). Rio de Janeiro: Padrão.

Mendonça, Renato. (1973). *A influência africana no português do Brasil* (4. ed.). Rio de Janeiro: Civilização Brasileira.

Milroy, L. (1997). *Observing and analysing natural language.* Oxford: Blackwell.

Oliveira, Marco Antônio. (1981). Reanálise de um problema de variação. In *PORTUGUÊS: estudos lingüísticos.* Uberaba: Centro de Ciências Humanas e Letras.

Oliveira, M. A. (1983). *Phonological variation and change in Brazilian Portuguese: The case of the liquids* (Doctoral dissertation). University of Pennsylvania, Philadelphia.

Oliveira, Marco A. (1991). The neogrammarian controversy revisited. *International Journal of the Sociology of Language*, 93-105.

Oliveira, Marco A. (1999). Reanalisando o processo de cancelamento do (r) em final de sílaba. *Revista de Estudos da Linguagem*, *6*, 31-58.

Phillips, Betty S. (2000). Lexical diffusion and competing analysis of sound change. In Donka Minkova & Robert Stockwell (Eds.), *Studies in the history of the English language: a millennial perspective* (pp. 231-243). Berlin: Mouton de Gruyter.

Santos, Theotonio. (1982). *Conceito de classes sociais.* Petrópolis: Vozes.

Schuchardt, Hugo. (1972). On sound laws: Against the neogrammarians and the transformational theory of phonological change. In Theo Venneman & Terence H. Wilbur, (Eds.), *Linguistiche Forschungen*, 26 (pp. 29-72). (Original work published in 1885). Frankfurt: Athenaeum.

Silva Neto, Serafim. (1938). *Fontes do latim vulgar:* Appendix Probi. Rio de Janeiro: Editora ABC.

Silva Neto, Serafim. (1986). *História da língua portuguesa no Brasil.* Rio de Janeiro: Presenca.

Stavrou, C. (1947). *Brazilian portuguese pronunciation.* Philadelphia: David Mackay Company.

Teyssier, Paul. (1990). *História da língua portuguesa.* Lisboa: Sá da Costa.

Trudgill, Peter. (1997). The social differenciation of English in Norwich. In N. Coupland & A. Jaworski (Eds.),*Sociolinguistics: A Reader and Coursebook (pp. 179-184).* Hampshire: Macmillian.

Votre, Sebastião. (1978). *Aspectos da variação fonológica na Fala do Rio de Janeiro* (Doctoral dissertation). Federal University of Rio de Janeiro, Rio de Janeiro.

Wang, William. (1969). Competing changes as a cause of residue. *Language,* 45, 9-25.

Wang, William. (1977). *The lexicon in phonological change.* The Hague: Mouton Publishers.

Wardhaugh, Ronald. (2002). *An introduction to sociolinguistics (4th ed.).* Oxford: Blackwell.

Wells, J.C. (1982). *Accents of English.* Cambridge: Cambridge University Press.

Weinreich, Uriel, Labov, William & Herzog, Marvin I. (1968). *Empirical foundations for a theory of language change.* In W.P. Lehman & Y. Malkiel (Eds.), *Directions for Historical Linguistics: A Symposium.* Austin: University of Texas Press.

Wray, A, Trott, K & Bloomer, A. (1998). *Projects in Linguistics. A practical guide to researching language.* London: Arnold.

Appendices

Appendix 1. Phonetic Transcription of R in Portuguese

Symbol	Classification of consonantal segment	Example	Phonetic Transcription	Observation
X	Fricative velar unvoiced	Rata	[Xata]	Pronunciation of people from Rio de Janeiro
		Marra	[MaXa]	
		Mar	[MaX]	
		Carta	[KaXta]	
ɣ	Fricative velar voiced	carga	[Kaɣga]	Pronunciation of people from Rio
h	Fricative glottal unvoiced	Rata	[hata]	Pronunciation of people from Belo Horizonte
		Marra	[maha]	
		Mar	[mah]	
		carta	[kahta]	
ɦ	Fricative glottal voiced	carga	[ka ɦga]	Pronunciation of people from Belo Horizonte
ɾ	Tepe alveolar voiced	Cara	[kaɾa]	Pronunciation of people from Portugal
		Prata	[pɾata]	
		Mar	[maɾ]	
		Carta	[kaɾta]	

ř	Vribante alveolar voiced	Rata marra	[řata] [mařa]	Pronunciation of people from Portugal and also from Sao Paulo, Brazil
	Retroflex alveolar voiced	mar	[mar]	Pronunciation of people from the country

Appendix 2. Statement of Privacy

Statement of Privacy / Permissão de uso

I understand this information that I provided is for the purposes a research done by Leonardo Reis. I give permission to take audio recordings of my voice and use it for its purpose.

Eu permito que a informação dada por mim para a pesquisa feita por Leonardo Reis seja utilizada. Também dou permissão para que minha voz seja gravada e que o uso seja para o propósito citado.

June 2013 / Junho 2013

Name/Nome: _____

Signature/Assinatura: _____

Date/Data: _____

Appendix 3. Informant Classification

Informant Classification / Classificacao do informante

1. Name/Nome: —————————————————————

2. Date of birth/Data de nascimento: ———————————————

3. Address/ Endereco: ——————————————————

   ——————————————————————————

4. Annual Income/ Salario Annual:

5. Education/Escolaridade:

Consent/Permissao

I allow this information to be used in this study.

Eu permito que a informação dada por mim seja usada nesta pesquisa.

June 2013 / Junho 2013

Signature/Assinatura: ————————————————————

Date/Data: ——————————————————

Appendix 4. Text Interview

Text:

A favor do amor à pátria

É Junho de 2006. Um mês não mais como outro **qualquer**. O mundo vive o **maior** evento esportivo de todos os tempos. Copa do Mundo na Alemanha. País triste que viveu anos de **horror** transforma toda **dor** em alegria. Esse é um **super** momento. Festa **popular** que reúne o **sonhador** do **interior** com o mais rico **imperador**.

O mundo inteiro está a **favor** do amor à Pátria. É momento de vestir a camisa da seleção. Hora que apenas um **líder**, representado por onze homens, será consagrado **martír** da alegria popular.

Os jogadores se preparam. Ouvem atentamente o **treinador** que fala de **amor** a camisa e clama por **prazer** em jogar bola. Todos param em frente à tela da televisão. A **mulher** não limpa mais o **lar**. O **trabalhador** esquece que amanhã é outro dia de trabalho. Até a **flor** fica mais colorida contagiada pelo **prazer** do **telespectador** que vibra a cada gol e a cada grito do **narrador**.

Obs. All non-verbal words highlighted have a final R, however, they were not highlighted when the informants read the passage.

Appendix 5. List of Words Interview

1	Moon / lua	22	Sky / Céu
2	Floor / Chão	23	**Worse / Pior**
3	**Bigger / maior**	24	Friend / amigo
4	**Lamp / Abajur**	25	**Any /qualquer**
5	Falt / falta	26	Heart / Coracao
6	**Sea / Mar**	27	**Pain / dor**
7	Second / segundo	28	Natural / natural
8	River / rio	29	**By / por**
9	**Super / super**	30	Fashion / moda
10	Time / tempo	31	**Woman / mulher**
11	**Femur / fémur**	32	**Place / lugar**
12	Romance / romance	33	Table / mesa
13	Girl / menina	34	Car / carro
14	**Dreamer / sonhador**	35	**Computer / computador**
15	Keyboard / teclado	36	Tree / arvore
16	Father / pai	37	England / Inglaterra
17	**Minor / menor**	38	**Researcher / pesquisador**
18	Brazilian / brasileiro	39	**Air / ar**
19	First / primeiro	40	**Cancer / câncer**
20	**Hero / mártir**	41	Victory / vitória
21	**Pair / par**	42	Brazil / Brasil

Obs. All non-verbal words highlighted have a final R; however, they were not highlighted and the informants read this list. The translation did not appear in the interview.

The method that I used to transcribe spoken data was simple. For the informal interview, I only wrote sentences where there was an occurrence of final R in non-verbal words. For the passage, I divided the text in 12 lines; if the informant deleted the R, I would rewrite the sentence, which I have numbered. For the word list, I only wrote the ones they have deleted the R.

I also translated the data to English because it was collected in Brazilian Portuguese. This is how I numbered the text:

Title: A <u>favor</u> do amor à pátria

1. É Junho de 2006. Um mês não mais como outro qualquer. O mundo vive o

2. maior evento esportivo de todos os tempos. Copa do Mundo na Alemanha. País triste .

3. que viveu anos de horror transforma toda dor em alegria. Esse é um super momento.

4. Festa popular que reúne o sonhador do interior com o mais rico imperador.

5. O mundo inteiro está a favor do amor à Pátria. É momento de vestir a camisa

6. da seleção. Hora que apenas um líder, representado por onze homens, será consagrado

7. màrtir da alegria popular.

8. Os jogadores se preparam. Ouvem atentamente o treinador que fala de amor a camisa

9. e clama por prazer em jogar bola. Todos param em frente à tela da televisão.

10. A mulher não limpa mais o lar. O trabalhador esquece que amanhã é outro dia de

11. trabalho. Até a flor fica mais colorida contagiada pelo prazer do telespectador que.

12. vibra a cada gol e a cada grito do narrador.

Appendix 6. Transcription Methods

Appendix 6.1. Informant Y

Informant: Y

Lower class

15-25 years old

Name: Denis – 21 years old

1. **Informal interview**

#	Transcription	Portuguese translated to English
1	Maior que antes	bigger than before
2	**Mulhe/ø/** gosta mais de tv	woman likes more tv
3	Pior eu não sou	I am not the worst
4	**Maio/ø/** não	ot bigger
5	**Computado/ø/** é da minha irmã	My sister's computer
6	Escola **partícula/ø/** é mais cara	Private school is more expensive
7	Minha cor favorita e verde	My favourite color is green
8	O **comprado/ø/** é quem paga mais	The customer is who spend more
9	Vestibular é muito difícil	Vestibular is very difficult
10	Lar é minha vida	Home is my life
11	Lugar bom de morar	A good place to live
12	Mar bom é do rio	Good beaches are in R
13	Itamar foi presidente	Itamar was president
14	O **vendedo/ø/** se não vender perde o emprego	if the Salesman doesn't sell he looses his job
15	**Junio/ø/** seria o nome dele	Júnior would be his name
16	Menor que 18 anos	Younger than 18 years old
17	Jogador de futebol	Football player

2. **Text reading**

Title: A <u>favor</u> do <u>amor</u> à pátria

1. É Junho de 2006. Um mês não mais como outro **qualquer**. O mundo vive o.

2. **<u>maior</u>** <u>evento</u> esportivo de todos os tempos. Copa do Mundo na Alemanha. País triste .

3. que viveu anos de **<u>horror</u>** <u>transforma</u> toda dor em alegria. Esse é um super momento.

4. O mundo inteiro está a **<u>favor</u>** do **<u>amor</u>** à Pátria. É momento de vestir a camisa 8.Os jogadores se preparam. Ouvem atentamente o **<u>treinador</u>** <u>que</u> fala de amor a camisa.

3. **Word list reading**

Mártir – marti/ø/ – hero

Appendix 6.2. Informant W

Informant: W

Lower class

15-25 years old

Name: Douglas – 22 years old

1. Informal Interview

#	Transcription	Translated to English
1	Maior que antes	bigger than before
2	**Mulhe/ø/** gosta mais de tv	woman likes more tv
3	Pior eu não sou	I am not the worst
4	Maior não	ot bigger
5	**Computado/ ø/** é da minha irmã	My sister's computer
6	Apesar que é mais cara	Although is more expensive
7	Minha cor favorita e verde	My favourite color is green
8	O **comprado/ø/** é quem paga mais	The customer is who spend more
9	Vestibular é muito difícil	Vestibular is very difficult
10	Lar é minha vida	Home is my life
11	**Luga/ø/** bom de morar	A good place to live
12	Mar bom é do rio	Good beaches are in Rio

2. **Text Reading**

Title: A <u>favor</u> do amor à pátria

1. É Junho de 2006. Um mês não mais como outro **qualquer**. O mundo vive o

2. **maior** <u>evento</u> esportivo de todos os tempos. Copa do Mundo na Alemanha. País triste.

3. mulher não limpa mais o lar. O **<u>trabalhador</u>** <u>esquece</u> que amanhã é outro dia de

4. trabalho. Até a flor fica mais colorida contagiada pelo prazer do **<u>telespectador</u>** <u>que</u>

3. **Word List Reading**

   * No final R deletion

Appendix 6.3. Informant R

Informant: R

Lower class

26-45 years old

Name: Junior – 29 years old

1. Informal Interview

#	Transcription	Translated to English
1	**Maio/ø/** que antes	bigger than before
2	Melhor que antes	Better than before
3	Eu frequento bar na cidade	I go to bars in the city
4	**Interio/ø/** de minas	Small cities in Minas
5	Pode ser na anterior	It can be the on before
6	Barman ganham bem	Barmen make good money
7	Particular	Escola partícula/ ø/ é mais cara
8	Por favor	please
9	**Computado/ø/** é muito caro	The computer is expensive
10	O **comprado/ø/** esta sempre certo	The customer is always right
11	**Vendedo/ø/** tem que vender	Salespeople must sell

2. **Text Reading**

Title: A <u>favor</u> do amor à pátria

1. **<u>maior</u>** <u>evento</u> esportivo de todos os tempos. Copa do Mundo na Alemanha. País triste.

2. que viveu anos de **<u>horror</u>** <u>transforma</u> toda dor em alegria. Esse é um super momento.

3. O mundo inteiro está a favor do amor à Pátria. É momento de vestir a camisa

4. **<u>mártir</u>** <u>da</u> alegria popular.

5. Os jogadores se preparam. Ouvem atentamente o **<u>treinador</u>** <u>que</u> fala de amor a camisa

3. **Word List Reading**

  * No final R deletion

Appendix 6.4. Informant S

Informant: S

Lower class

26-45 years old

Name: Márcio – 28 years old

1. Informal Interview

#	Transcription	Translated to English
1	Maior que antes	bigger than before
2	**Mulhe/ø/** é mais	Woman is more
3	**Mulhe/ø/** do que homem	Woman than man
4	**Interio/ø/** de minas	Small cities in Minas
5	Lar é familia	Home is family
6	**Computado/ø/** é muito caro	Computer is more expensive
7	Itamar Franco	Itamar Franco
8	**Computado/ø/** tem que ser bom	It has to be a good computer
9	**Consumido/ø/** é muito enganado	The customer is cheated
10	**Vendedo/ø/** tem que vender	Salesman has to sell
11	**Junio/ø/** é meu irmao	Junior is my brother
12	Melhor de morar	Beter than live

2. Text Reading

1. que viveu anos de **horror** transforma toda dor em alegria. Esse é um super momento.

2. **mártir** da alegria popular.

3. Word List Reading

* No final R deletion

Appendix 6.5. Informant H

Informant: H

Lower class

46-60 years old

Name: Nautilus – 54 years old

1. Informal Interview

#	Transcription	Translated to English
1	Bem maior que antes	Even bigger than before
2	Mais mulhe/ø/ que homem	More woman than man
3	Não frequento bar	I don't go to bar
4	60% vem do interior de minas	60% come from the country
5	Ter um lar é importante	It is important to have a home
6	Sei nada de computador	I know nothing about computer
7	Cobrado/ø/ de onibus	Cashier on the bus
8	Doutor e quem tem dinheiro	Doctos is who have a lot money
9	Particula/ø/ so pra rico	Private school is for the rich
10	Computado/ø/ é caro	Computer is expensive
11	Comprado/ø/ não tem grana	Customer don't have money
12	Ser vendedo/ø/ e dificil	It's difficult to be a salesman

2. Text Reading

2. **maior** evento esportivo de todos os tempos. Copa do Mundo na Alemanha. País triste.

7. **mártir** da alegria popular.

3. Word List Reading

Marti/ ø/

Informant: F

Lower class

46-60 years old

Name: Estaurina – 46 years old

1. Informal Interview

#	Transcription	Translated to English
1	Maior que antes	bigger than before
2	Pior que não tenho	The worse par tis that i don't have
3	Bar e bom demais	Bar is so goodWoman than man
4	Minha cor e rosa	My favourite color is pink
5	**Interio/ø/** não tem violencia	There is no violence in the country
6	Lar e Deus	Home is God
7	Partícular so pra rico	Private school only for the rich
8	**Melho/ø/** bairro e pampulha	The best area is Pampulha
9	**Computado/ø/** e lap top?	Computer is lap top?
10	**Vendedo/ø/** tem que vender	Salesman has to sell
11	Meu primo e Junior	My cousin is Junior
12	Comprador da FIAT	He is a buyer at FIAT

2. Text Reading

1. É Junho de 2006. Um mês não mais como outro **qualquer**. O mundo vive o

3. Word List Reading

* No final R deletion

Appendix 6.7. Informant G

Informant: G

Middle Class

46-60 years old

Name: Edgar – 58 years old

1. Informal Interview

#	Transcription	Translated to English
1	Maior que antes	bigger than before
2	Tem mais mulher ne?	There is more woman, isn't it?
3	cada vez mais pior	It is getting worse
4	Minha cor e vermelho	My color is red
5	Celular facilita muito	A mobile makes your life easier
6	Maior parte das pessoas	The majority of the population
7	Das cidades do interior	From the smaller cities
8	Lar e onde vc tem sua familia	Home is where you family is
9	Corrector ganha bem	Who sells properties make good money
10	Professor ganha mal	Teacher don't have a good salary

2. Text Reading

*No final R deletion in the text

3. Word List Reading

* No final R deletion in the word list

Appendix 6.8. Informant P

Informant: P

Middle Class

46-60 years old

Name: Lucia – 60 years old

1. Informal Interview

#	Transcription	Translated to English
1	**Maio/ø/** que antes	bigger than before
2	Acho que e mulher	I think it is woman
3	Melhor em termos de tecnologia	Better in terms of technology
4	Esta pior devido a violencia	It is worse because of the violence
5	O **celula/ø/** esta mais acessivel	It is easier to buy a mobile
6	Lar e o aconchego da familia	Home is the relief of a family
7	Computador e um saco	I hate computer
8	O professor merece mais respeito	Teachers deserve more respect
9	Ser trocador e profissão de risco	It is risk to be a busdriver
10	Jogador ganha muito bem	Footbal player makes a lot of money

2. Text Reading

*No final R deletion in the text

3. Word List Reading

* No final R deletion in the word list

Appendix 6.9. Informant K

Informant: K

Middle Class

15-25 years old

Name: Cristiane – 24 years old

1. Informal Interview

#	Transcription	Translated to English
1	O **direto/ø/** da faculdade	The director of my college
2	Acho que e mulher	I think it is woman
3	Melhor em quase tudo	Better in almsot everything
4	Pra ter celular tem que saber usar	you must know how to use it a mobile
5	Corrector de imoveis ganha bem	Property salesman makes good money
6	O **computado/ø/** e essencial	Computer is essencial
7	Itamar foi um bom presidente	Itamar was a good president
8	A particular e melhor	Private is better
9	Consumidor esta bem protegido	The customer is protect by law
10	O **pio/ø/e** roubar e não levar	The worst is to steal and don't take it
11	Interior de mias e mais seguro	The country is safer than the city
12	**Melho/ø/** em campo foi o kaka	The best in the pitch was kaka
13	Adoro ver o mar de noite	I love to see the sea at night

2. Text Reading

*No final R deletion in the text

3. Word List Reading

* No final R deletion in the word list

Informant: X

Middle Class

26-45 years old

Name: Celia – 41 years old

1. Informal Interview

#	Transcription	Translated to English
1	A flor do meu jardim	The flour in the garden
2	Acho que e mulher	I think it is woman
3	Melhor em quase tudo	Better in almost everything
4	Pra ter celular tem que saber usar	you must know how to use it a mobile
5	No exterior voce encontra de tudo	Overseas you can find everything
6	O computador e essencial	Computer is essencial
7	E o provedor	And the provider
8	Ventilador de teto	Ceileing ventilator
9	O contador que faz isso	The account who does it
10	**Douto/ø/** e quem tem doutorado	Doctor is whom have a doctor degree
11	Professor e medico	Teacher and doctor
12	O ar fica mais puro	The air is more pure

2. Text Reading

*No final R deletion in the text

3. Word List Reading

* No final R deletion in the word list

Appendix 6.11. Informant V

Informant: V

Middle Class

26-45 years old

Name: Yasline – 30 years old

1. Informal Interview

#	Transcription	Translated to English
1	O computador e essencial	Computer is essential
2	Acho que e **mulhe/ø/**	I think it is woman
3	Melhor em quase tudo	Better in almsot everything
4	Pra ter celular tem que saber usar	You must know how to use it a mobile
5	Apesar que nao	I don't think so
6	Por favor	Please
7	Meu supervisor	My supervisor
8	Pode ser pior	It can be worse
9	O servidor e quem garante	The supplier is who garantee
10	Professor e padre	Teacher and p the priest
11	O amor e carinho	Love and care

2. Text Reading

*No final R deletion in the text

3. Word List Reading

* No final R deletion in the word list

Appendix 6.12. Informant Z

Informant: Z

Middle class

15-25

Name: Bruno – 23 years old

1. Informal Interview

#	Transcription	Translated to English
1	**Maio/ø/** que antes	bigger than before
2	**Mulhe/ø/** broto e de minas	Nice woman only in Minas
3	Meu **celula/ø/** r e show	My mobile is top
4	A **maio/ø/** do mundo	The biggest in the world
5	**Vestibula/ø/** ta foda	Vestibular sucks
6	**Douto/ø/** e medico	Doctor is doctor
7	**Computado/ø/** e tudo hoje	Computer is everything today
8	O professor tem que saber ensinar	Teacher has to know how to teach
9	Ele e um bom jogador	He is a good player
10	Ele esta bem superior	He is way up
11	Apesar de ser campeao	Although he is champion

2. **Text Reading**

1. **<u>maior</u>** <u>evento</u> esportivo de todos os tempos. Copa do Mundo na Alemanha. País triste .

2. que viveu anos de **<u>horror</u>** <u>transforma</u> toda <u>dor em</u> alegria. Esse é um super momento.

3. **<u>màrtir</u>** <u>da</u> alegria popular.

4. Os jogadores se preparam. Ouvem atentamente o **<u>treinador</u>** <u>que</u> fala de amor a camisa.

5. **3. Word list reading**

   * No final R deletion in the word list

Appendix 7.Codification Key

1) R deletion	2) Number of syllabus	3) Following Word	4) Word class
D – delete N – non-delete	M – monossílaba P – polissílaba	V – Vowel C – Consonant P – Pause	S – Substantive A – adjective C – Connectives (preposition and adverb)
5) Style I – Informal T – Text L – Word list	**6) Social class** L – Lower M – Middle	**7) Age Group** A – 15-25 B – 26-45 C – 46-60	**8) Informants** **Y—Denis**
W – Douglas	**R—Junior**	**S—Marcio**	**H – Nautilus**
F—Estaurina	**G—Edgar**	**P—Lucia**	**Z—Bruno**
K—Cristiane	**X—Celia**	**V—Yasline**	

Appendix 7.1.Informant Y codification

Y = DENIS—21 – LOWER CLASS – (15-25)

Informal Interview

(NPCAILAY MAIOR—1
(DPCSILAY MULHEX—2 *
(DPCAILAY MAIOX—3 *
(DPVSILAY COMPUTADOX-4 *
(DPVSILAY COMPRADOX—5 *
(DPCSILAY VENDEDOX 6* (DPCSILAY JUNIOX—7 *
(DPVSILAY PARTICULAX—8 *
(NPVAILAY PIOR—9
(NMCSILAY COR—10
(NPVSILAY VESTIBULAR—11
(NMVSILAY LAR—12
(NPCSILAY LUGAR—13
(NMCSILAY MAR—14
(NPCSILAY ITAMAR—15
(NPCAILAY MENOR—16
(NPCSILAY JOGADOR—17

Text

(DPVATLAY MAIOX—1 *
(DPCSTLAY HORROX—2 *
(DPCSTLAY FAVOX—3 *
(DPVSTLAY AMOX—4 *
(DPCSTLAY TREINADOX—5 *
(DPCSTLAY MARTIX—6 *
(DPCSTLAY FAVOX—7 *
(DPVSTLAY AMOX—8 *
(NPPCTLAY QUALQUER—9
(NMVSTLAY DOR—10
(NPCATLAY SUPER—11
(NPCSTLAY POPULAR—12
(NPCSTLAY SONHADOR—13

(NPCSTLAY INTERIOR—14
(NPPSTLAY IMPERADOR—15
(NPCSTLAY LIDER—16
(NPCSTLAY MARTIR—17
(NPPATLAY POPULAR—18
(NMCCTLAY POR—19
(NPVSTLAY PRAZER—20
(NMPSTLAY LAR—21
(NPVSTLAY TRABALHADOR—22
(NMCSTLAY FLOR—23
(NPCSTLAY PRAZER—24
(NPCSTLAY TELESPECTADOR—25
(NPPSTLAY NARRADOR—26

Word List

(NPPALLAY MAIOR—1
(NPPSLLAY ABAJUR—2
(NMPSLLAY MAR—3
(NPPALLAY SUPER—4
(NPPSLLAY FEMUR—5
(NPPSLLAY SONHADOR—6
(NPPALLAY MENOR—7
(DPPSLLAY MARTIX—8 *
(NMPSLLAY PAR—9
(NPPALLAY PIOR—10
(NPPCLLAY QUALQUER—11
(NMPSLLAY DOR—12
(NMPCLLAY POR—13
(NPPSLLAY MULHER—14
(NPPSLLAY LUGAR—15
(NPPSLLAY COMPUTADOR—16
(NPPSLLAY PESQUISADOR—17
(NMPSLLAY AR—18
(NPPSLLAY CANCER—19

Appendix 7.2. Informant W codification

W = DOUGLAS—22 – LOWER CLASS – (15-25)

Informal Interview

(NPVAILAW MAIOR—1
(DPCSILAW MULHEX—2 *
(NPCAILAW PIOR—3
(NPCAILAW MAIOR—4
(DPCSILAW COMPUTADOX—5 *
(NPCCILAW APESAR—6
(DMCSILAW COX—7 *
(DPCSILAW COMPRADOX—8 *
(NPVSILAW VESTIBULAR—9
(NMCSILAW LAR—10
(DPVSILAW LUGAX—11 *
(NMCSILAW MAR—12

Text

(DPCSTLAW FAVOX—1 *
(NPVSTLAW AMOR—2
(DPPCTLAW QUALQUEX—3 *
(DPVATLAW MAIOX—4 *
(NPCSTLAW HORROR—5
(NMVSTLAW DOR—6
(NPCATLAW SUPER—7
(NPCSTLAW POPULAR—8
(NPPSTLAW SONHADOR—9
(NPCSTLAW INTERIOR—10
(NPPSTLAW IMPERADOR—11
(NPCSTLAW FAVOR—12
(NPVSTLAW AMOR—13
(NPCSTLAW LIDER—14
(NPCSTLAW MARTIR—15
(NPPATLAW POPULAR—16
(NPCSTLAW TREINADOR—17

(NPVSTLAW AMOR—18
(NMCCTLAW POR—19
(NPVSTLAW PRAZER—20
(NMPSTLAW LAR—21
(DPVSTLAW TRABALHADOX—22 *
(NMCSTLAW FLOR—23
(NPCSTLAW PRAZER—24
(DPCSTLAW TELESPECTADOX—25 *
(NPPSTLAW NARRADOR—26

Word List

(NPPALLAW MAIOR—1
(NPPSLLAW ABAJUR—2
(NMPSLLAW MAR—3
(NPPALLAW SUPER—4
(NPPSLLAW FEMUR—5
(NPPSLLAW SONHADOR—6
(NPPALLAW MENOR—7
(NPPSLLAW MARTIR—8
(NMPSLLAW PAR—9
(NPPALLAW PIOR—10
(NPPCLLAW QUALQUER—11
(NMPSLLAW DOR—12
(NMPCLLAW POR—13
(NPPSLLAW MULHER—14
(NPPSLLAW LUGAR—15
(NPPSLLAW COMPUTADOR—16
(NPPSLLAW PESQUISADOR—17
(NMPSLLAW AR—18
(NPPSLLAW CANCER—19

Appendix 7.3. Informant Z codification

Z = BRUNO—23 – MIDDLE CLASS – (15-25)

Informal Interview

(DPCAIMAZ MAIOX—1 *
(NPCCIMAZ APESAR—2
(DPCSIMAZ MULHEX—3 *
(DPVSIMAZ CELULAX—4 *
(DPCAIMAZ MAIOX—5 *
(DPCSIMAZ VESTIBULAX—6 *
(DPVSIMAZ DOUTOX—7 *
(DPVSIMAZ COMPUTADOX—8 *
(NPCSIMAZ PROFESSOR—9
(NPCSIMAZ JOGADOR—10
(NPPSIMAZ SUPERIOR—11

Text

(NPCSTMAZ FAVOR—1
(NPVSTMAZ AMOR—2
(NPPCTMAZ QUALQUER—3
(DPVATMAZ MAIOX—4 *
(DPCSTMAZ HORROX—5 *
(DMVSTMAZ DOX—6 *
(NPCATMAZ SUPER—7
(NPCSTMAZ POPULAR—8
(NPPSTMAZ SONHADOR—9
(NPCSTMAZ INTERIOR—10
(NPPSTMAZ IMPERADOR—11
(NPCSTMAZ FAVOR—12
(NPVSTMAZ AMOR—13
(NPCSTMAZ LIDER—14
(DPCSTMAZ MARTIX—15 *
(NPPATMAZ POPULAR—16
(DPCSTMAZ TREINADOX—17 *
(NPVSTMAZ AMOR—18

(NMCCTMAZ POR—19
(NPVSTMAZ PRAZER—20
(NMPSTMAZ LAR—21
(NPVSTMAZ TRABALHADOR—22
(NMCSTMAZ FLOR—23
(NPCSTMAZ PRAZER—24
(NPCSTMAZ TELESPECTADOR—25
(NPPSTMAZ NARRADOR—26

Word List

(NPPALMAZ MAIOR—1
(NPPSLMAZ ABAJUR—2
(NMPSLMAZ MAR—3
(NPPALMAZ SUPER—4
(NPPSLMAZ FEMUR—5
(NPPSLMAZ SONHADOR—6
(NPPALMAZ MENOR—7
(NPPSLMAZ MARTIR—8
(NMPSLMAZ PAR—9
(NPPALMAZ PIOR—10
(NPPCLMAZ QUALQUER—11
(NMPSLMAZ DOR—12
(NMPCLMAZ POR—13
(NPPSLMAZ MULHER—14
(NPPSLMAZ LUGAR—15
(NPPSLMAZ COMPUTADOR—16
(NPPSLMAZ PESQUISADOR—17
(NMPSLMAZ AR—18
(NPPSLMAZ CANCER—19

Appendix 7.4. Informant K codification

K = CRISTIANE—24 – MIDDLE CLASS – (15-25)

Informal Interview

(DPCSIMAK DIRETOX—1 *
(NPPSIMAK MULHER—2
(DPVAIMAK MELHOX—3 *
(NPCSIMAK CELULAR—4
(NPCSIMAK CORRETOR—5
(DPVSIMAK COMPUTADOX—6 *
(NPCSIMAK ITAMAR—7
(NPVSIMAK PARTICULAR—8
(NPPAIMAK MELHOR—9
(NPVSIMAK CONSUMIDOR—10
(DPVAIMAK PIOX—11 *
(NPCSIMAK INTERIOR—12
(DPVAIMAK MELHOX—13 *
(NMCSIMAK MAR—14

Text

(NPCSTMAK FAVOR—1
(NPVSTMAK AMOR—2
(NPPCTMAK QUALQUER—3
(NPVATMAK MAIOR—4
(NPCSTMAK HORROR—5
(NMVSTMAK DOR—6
(NPCATMAK SUPER—7
(NPCSTMAK POPULAR—8
(NPPSTMAK SONHADOR—9
(NPCSTMAK INTERIOR—10
(NPPSTMAK IMPERADOR—11
(NPCSTMAK FAVOR—12
(NPVSTMAK AMOR—13
(NPCSTMAK LIDER—14
(NPCSTMAK MARTIR—15

(NPPATMAK POPULAR—16
(NPCSTMAK TREINADOR—17
(NPVSTMAK AMOR—18
(NMCCTMAK POR—19
(NPVSTMAK PRAZER—20
(NMPSTMAK LAR—21
(NPVSTMAK TRABALHADOR—22
(NMCSTMAK FLOR—23
(NPCSTMAK PRAZER—24
(NPCSTMAK TELESPECTADOR—25
(NPPSTMAK NARRADOR—26

Word List

(NPPALMAK MAIOR—1
(NPPSLMAK ABAJUR—2
(NMPSLMAK MAR—3
(NPPALMAK SUPER—4
(NPPSLMAK FEMUR—5
(NPPSLMAK SONHADOR—6
(NPPALMAK MENOR—7
(NPPSLMAK MARTIR—8
(NMPSLMAK PAR—9
(NPPALMAK PIOR—10
(NPPCLMAK QUALQUER—11
(NMPSLMAK DOR—12
(NMPCLMAK POR—13
(NPPSLMAK MULHER—14
(NPPSLMAK LUGAR—15
(NPPSLMAK COMPUTADOR—16
(NPPSLMAK PESQUISADOR—17
(NMPSLMAK AR—18
(NPPSLMAK CANCER—19

Appendix 7.5. Informant V codification

V = YASLINE—30 – MIDDLE CLASS – (26-45)

Informal Interview

(NPVSIMBV COMPUTADOR—1
(DPPSIMBV MULHEX—2 *
(NPVAIMBV MELHOR—3
(NPCSIMBV CELULAR—4
(NPCCIMBV APESAR—5
(NMVCIMBV POR—6
(NPPSIMBV SUPERVISOR—7
(NPVSIMBV SERVIDOR—8
(NPVSIMBV PROFESSOR—9
(NPVSIMBV AMOR—10
(NPCAIMBV PIOR—11

Text

(NPCSTMBV FAVOR—1
(NPVSTMBV AMOR—2
(NPPCTMBV QUALQUER—3
(NPVATMBV MAIOR—4
(NPCSTMBV HORROR—5
(NMVSTMBV DOR—6
(NPCATMBV SUPER—7
(NPCSTMBV POPULAR—8
(NPPSTMBV SONHADOR—9
(NPCSTMBV INTERIOR—10
(NPPSTMBV IMPERADOR—11
(NPCSTMBV FAVOR—12
(NPVSTMBV AMOR—13
(NPCSTMBV LIDER—14
(NPCSTMBV MARTIR—15
(NPPATMBV POPULAR—16
(NPCSTMBV TREINADOR—17
(NPVSTMBV AMOR—18

(NMCCTMBV POR—19
(NPVSTMBV PRAZER—20
(NMPSTMBV LAR—21
(NPVSTMBV TRABALHADOR—22
(NMCSTMBV FLOR—23
(NPCSTMBV PRAZER—24
(NPCSTMBV TELESPECTADOR—25
(NPPSTMBV NARRADOR—26

Word List

(NPPALMBV MAIOR—1
(NPPSLMBV ABAJUR—2
(NMPSLMBV MAR—3
(NPPALMBV SUPER—4
(NPPSLMBV FEMUR—5
(NPPSLMBV SONHADOR—6
(NPPALMBV MENOR—7
(NPPSLMBV MARTIR—8
(NMPSLMBV PAR—9
(NPPALMBV PIOR—10
(NPPCLMBV QUALQUER—11
(NMPSLMBV DOR—12
(NMPCLMBV POR—13
(NPPSLMBV MULHER—14
(NPPSLMBV LUGAR—15
(NPPSLMBV COMPUTADOR—16
(NPPSLMBV PESQUISADOR—17
(NMPSLMBV AR—18
(NPPSLMBV CANCER—19

Appendix 7.6. Informant X codification

X = CELIA – 41 – MIDDLE CLASS – (26-45)

Informal Interview

(NMCSIMBX FLOR—1
(NPPSIMBX MULHER—2
(NPVAIMBX MELHOR—3
(NPCSIMBX CELULAR—4
(NPCSIMBX EXTERIOR—5
(NPPSIMBX COMPUTADOR—6
(NPPSIMBX PROVEDOR—7
(NPCSIMBX VENTILADOR—8
(NPCSIMBX CONTADOR—9
(DPVSIMBX DOUTOX—10 *
(NPVSIMBX PROFESSOR—11
(NMCSIMBX AR—12

Text

(NPCSTMBX FAVOR –1
(NPVSTMBX AMOR—2
(NPPCTMBX QUALQUER—3
(NPVATMBX MAIOR—4
(NPCSTMBX HORROR—5
(NMVSTMBX DOR—6
(NPCATMBX SUPER—7
(NPCSTMBX POPULAR—8
(NPPSTMBX SONHADOR—9
(NPCSTMBX INTERIOR—10
(NPPSTMBX IMPERADOR—11
(NPCSTMBX FAVOR—12
(NPVSTMBX AMOR—13
(NPCSTMBX LIDER—14
(NPCSTMBX MARTIR—15
(NPPATMBX POPULAR—16
(NPCSTMBX TREINADOR—17

(NPVSTMBX AMOR—18
(NMCCTMBX POR—19
(NPVSTMBX PRAZER—20
(NMPSTMBX LAR—21
(NPVSTMBX TRABALHADOR—22
(NMCSTMBX FLOR—23
(NPCSTMBX PRAZER—24
(NPCSTMBX TELESPECTADOR—25
(NPPSTMBX NARRADOR –26

Word List

(NPPALMBX MAIOR—1
(NPPSLMBX ABAJUR—2
(NMPSLMBX MAR—3
(NPPALMBX SUPER—4
(NPPSLMBX FEMUR—5
(NPPSLMBX SONHADOR—6
(NPPALMBX MENOR—7
(NPPSLMBX MARTIR—8
(NMPSLMBX PAR—9
(NPPALMBX PIOR—10
(NPPCLMBX QUALQUER—11
(NMPSLMBX DOR—12
(NMPCLMBX POR—13
(NPPSLMBX MULHER—14
(NPPSLMBX LUGAR—15
(NPPSLMBX COMPUTADOR—16
(NPPSLMBX PESQUISADOR—17
(NMPSLMBX AR—18
(NPPSLMBX CANCER—19

Appendix 7.7. Informant S codification

S = MARCIO—28 – LOWER CLASS – (25-45)

Informal Interview

(NPCAILBS MAIOR—1
(DPCSILBS MULHEX—2 *
(DPCSILBS MULHEX—3 *
(DPCSILBS INTERIOX—4 *
(NMVSILBS LAR—5
(DPVSILBS COMPUTADOX—6 *
(NPCSILBS ITAMAR—7
(DPCSILBS COMPUTADOX—8 *
(DPCSILBS CONSUMIDOX—9 *
(DPCSILBS VENDEDOX—10 *
(DPVSILBS JUNIOX—11 *
(NPCSILBS MELHOR—12

Text

(NPCSTLBS FAVOR—1
(NPVSTLBS AMOR—2
(NPPCTLBS QUALQUER—3
(NPVATLBS MAIOR—4
(DPCSTLBS HORROX—5 *
(NMVSTLBS DOR—6
(NPCATLBS SUPER—7
(NPCSTLBS POPULAR—8
(NPPSTLBS SONHADOR—9
(NPCSTLBS INTERIOR—10
(NPPSTLBS IMPERADOR—11
(NPCSTLBS FAVOR—12
(NPVSTLBS AMOR—13
(NPCSTLBS LIDER—14
(DPCSTLBS MARTIX—15 *
(NPPATLBS POPULAR—16
(NPCSTLBS TREINADOR—17

(NPVSTLBS AMOR—18
(NMCCTLBS POR—19
(NPVSTLBS PRAZER—20
(NMPSTLBS LAR—21
(NPVSTLBS TRABALHADOR—22
(NMCSTLBS FLOR—23
(NPCSTLBS PRAZER –24
(NPCSTLBS TELESPECTADOR –25
(NPPSTLBS NARRADOR—26

Word List

(NPPALLBS MAIOR—1
(NPPSLLBS ABAJUR—2
(NMPSLLBS MAR—3
(NPPALLBS SUPER –4
(NPPSLLBS FEMUR—5
(NPPSLLBS SONHADOR—6
(NPPALLBS MENOR—7
(NPPSLLBS MARTIR—8
(NMPSLLBS PAR—9
(NPPALLBS PIOR—10
(NPPCLLBS QUALQUER—11
(NMPSLLBS DOR—12
(NMPCLLBS POR—13
(NPPSLLBS MULHER—14
(NPPSLLBS LUGAR—15
(NPPSLLBS COMPUTADOR—16
(NPPSLLBS PESQUISADOR—17
(NMPSLLBS AR—18
(NPPSLLBS CANCER—19

Appendix 7.8. Informant R codification

R = JUNIOR—29 – LOWER CLASS – (25-45)

Informal Interview

(DPCAILBR MAIOX—1 *
(NPCSILBR MELHOR—2
(NMCSILBR BAR—3
(NPCSILBR INTERIOR—4
(NPCSILBR BARMAN—5
(NPCSILBR PARTICULAR—6
(DPVSILBR COMPUTADOX—7 *
(DPVSILBR COMPRADOX—8 *
(DPCSILBR VENDEDOX—9 *
(DPCSILBR ANTERIOX—10 *
(NMVSILBR POR—11

Text

(DPCSTLBR FAVOX—1 *
(NPVSTLBR AMOR—2
(NPPCTLBR QUALQUER—3
(DPVATLBR MAIOX—4 *
(DPCSTLBR HORROX—5 *
(NMVSTLBR DOR—6
(NPCATLBR SUPER—7
(NPCSTLBR POPULAR—8
(NPPSTLBR SONHADOR—9
(NPCSTLBR INTERIOR—10
(NPPSTLBR IMPERADOR—11
(DPCSTLBR FAVOX—12 *
(NPVSTLBR AMOR—13
(NPCSTLBR LIDER—14
(DPCSTLBR MARTIX—15 *
(NPPATLBR POPULAR—16
(DPCSTLBR TREINADOX—17 *
(NPVSTLBR AMOR—18

(NMCCTLBR POR—19
(NPVSTLBR PRAZER –20
(NMPSTLBR LAR—21
(NPVSTLBR TRABALHADOR—22
(NMCSTLBR FLOR—23
(NPCSTLBR PRAZER—24
(NPCSTLBR TELESPECTADOR—25
(NPPSTLBR NARRADOR –26

Word List

(NPPALLBR MAIOR—1
(NPPSLLBR ABAJUR—2
(NMPSLLBR MAR—3
(NPPALLBR SUPER—4
(NPPSLLBR FEMUR—5
(NPPSLLBR SONHADOR—6
(NPPALLBR MENOR—7
(NPPSLLBR MARTIR—8
(NMPSLLBR PAR—9
(NPPALLBR PIOR—10
(NPPCLLBR QUALQUER—11
(NMPSLLBR DOR—12
(NMPCLLBR POR—13
(NPPSLLBR MULHER—14
(NPPSLLBR LUGAR—15
(NPPSLLBR COMPUTADOR—16
(NPPSLLBR PESQUISADOR—17
(NMPSLLBR AR—18
(NPPSLLBR CANCER—19

Appendix 7.9. Informant G codification

G = EDGAR—58 – MIDDLE CLASS – (46-60)

Informal Interview

(NPCAIMCG MAIOR—1
(NPCCIMCG MULHER—2
(NPPSIMCG PIOR—3
(NMVSIMCG COR 4
(NPCSIMCG CELULAR—5
(NPCAIMCG MAIOR—6
(NPPSIMCG INTERIOR—7
(NMVSIMCG LAR—8
(NPCSIMCG CORRETOR—9
(NPCSIMCG PROFESSOR—10

Text

(NPCSTMCG FAVOR—1
(NPVSTMCG AMOR—2
(NPPCTMCG QUALQUER—3
(NPVATMCG MAIOR—4
(NPCSTMCG HORROR—5
(NMVSTMCG DOR—6
(NPCATMCG SUPER—7
(NPCSTMCG POPULAR—8
(NPPSTMCG SONHADOR—9
(NPCSTMCG INTERIOR—10
(NPPSTMCG IMPERADOR—11
(NPCSTMCG FAVOR—12
(NPVSTMCG AMOR—13
(NPCSTMCG LIDER—14
(NPCSTMCG MARTIR—15
(NPPATMCG POPULAR—16
(NPCSTMCG TREINADOR—17
(NPVSTMCG AMOR—18
(NMCCTMCG POR—19

(NPVSTMCG PRAZER—20
(NMPSTMCG LAR—21
(NPVSTMCG TRABALHADOR—22
(NMCSTMCG FLOR—23
(NPCSTMCG PRAZER—24
(NPCSTMCG TELESPECTADOR—25
(NPPSTMCG NARRADOR—26

Word List

(NPPALMCG MAIOR—1
(NPPSLMCG ABAJUR—2
(NMPSLMCG MAR—3
(NPPALMCG SUPER—4
(NPPSLMCG FEMUR—5
(NPPSLMCG SONHADOR—6
(NPPALMCG MENOR—7
(NPPSLMCG MARTIR—8
(NMPSLMCG PAR—9
(NPPALMCG PIOR—10
(NPPCLMCG QUALQUER—11
(NMPSLMCG DOR—12
(NMPCLMCG POR—13
(NPPSLMCG MULHER—14
(NPPSLMCG LUGAR—15
(NPPSLMCG COMPUTADOR—16
(NPPSLMCG PESQUISADOR—17
(NMPSLMCG AR—18
(NPPSLMCG CANCER—19

Appendix 7.10. Informant P codification

P = LUCIA—60 – MIDDLE CLASS – (46-60)

Informal Interview

(NPVAIMCP MAIOR—1
(NPPCIMCP MULHER—2
(NPCSIMCP MELHOR—3
(NPCSIMCP PIOR—4
(DPCSIMCP CELULAX—5 *
(NMVSIMCP LAR—6
(NPPSIMCP COMPUTADOR—7
(NPPSIMCP PROFESSOR—8
(NPPSIMCP TROCADOR—9
(NPPSIMCP JOGADOR—10

Text

(NPCSTMCP FAVOR—1
(NPVSTMCP AMOR—2
(NPPCTMCP QUALQUER—3
(NPVATMCP MAIOR—4
(NPCSTMCP HORROR—5
(NMVSTMCP DOR—6
(NPCATMCP SUPER—7
(NPCSTMCP POPULAR—8
(NPPSTMCP SONHADOR—9
(NPCSIMCP INTERIOR—10
(NPPSIMCP IMPERADOR—11
(NPCSTMCP FAVOR—12
(NPVSTMCP AMOR—13
(NPCSTMCP LIDER—14
(NPCSTMCP MARTIR—15
(NPPATMCP POPULAR—16
(NPCSTMCP TREINADOR—17
(NPVSTMCP AMOR—18
(NMCCTMCP POR—19

(NPVSTMCP PRAZER—20
(NMPSTMCP LAR—21
(NPVSTMCP TRABALHADOR—22
(NMCSTMCP FLOR—23
(NPCSTMCP PRAZER—24
(NPCSTMCP TELESPECTADOR—25
(NPPSTMCP NARRADOR—26

Word List

(NPPALMCP MAIOR—1
(NPPSLMCP ABAJUR—2
(NMPSLMCP MAR—3
(NPPALMCP SUPER—4
(NPPSLMCP FEMUR—5
(NPPSLMCP SONHADOR—6
(NPPALMCP MENOR—7
(NPPSLMCP MARTIR—8
(NMPSLMCP PAR—9
(NPPALMCP PIOR—10
(NPPCLMCP QUALQUER—11
(NMPSLMCP DOR—12
(NMPCLMCP POR—13
(NPPSLMCP MULHER—14
(NPPSLMCP LUGAR—15
(NPPSLMCP COMPUTADOR—16
(NPPSLMCP PESQUISADOR—17
(NMPSLMCP AR—18
(NPPSLMCP CANCER—19

Appendix 7.11. Informant H codification

H = NAUTILUS—54 – LOWER CLASS – (46-60)

Informal Interview

(NPCAILCH MAIOR—1
(DPCSILCH MULHEX—2 *
(NMPSILCH BAR—3
(NPCSILCH INTERIOR—4
(NMVSILCH LAR—5
(NPPSILCH COMPUTADOR—6
(DPCSILCH COBRADOX—7 *
(NPVSILCH DOUTOR—8
(DPCSILCH PARTICULAX—9 *
(DPVSILCH COMPUTADOX—10 *
(DPCSILCH COMPRADOX—11 *
(DPVSILCH VENDEDOX—12 *

Text

(NPCSTLCH FAVOR—1
(NPVSTLCH AMOR—2
(NPPCTLCH QUALQUER—3
(DPVATLCH MAIOX—4 *
(NPCSTLCH HORROR—5
(NMVSTLCH DOR—6
(NPCATLCH SUPER—7
(NPCSTLCH POPULAR—8
(NPPSTLCH SONHADOR—9
(NPCSTLCH INTERIOR—10
(NPPSTLCH IMPERADOR—11
(NPCSTLCH FAVOR—12
(NPVSTLCH AMOR—13
(NPCSTLCH LIDER—14
(DPCSTLCH MARTIX—15 *
(NPPATLCH POPULAR—16
(NPCSTLCH TREINADOR—17

(NPVSTLCH AMOR—18
(NMCCTLCH POR—19
(NPVSTLCH PRAZER—20
(NMPSTLCH LAR—21
(NPVSTLCH TRABALHADOR—22
(NMCSTLCH FLOR—23
(NPCSTLCH PRAZER—24
(NPCSTLCH TELESPECTADOR—25
(NPPSTLCH NARRADOR—26

Word List

(NPPALLCH MAIOR—1
(NPPSLLCH ABAJUR—2
(NMPSLLCH MAR—3
(NPPALLCH SUPER—4
(NPPSLLCH FEMUR—5
(NPPSLLCH SONHADOR—6
(NPPALLCH MENOR—7
(DPPSLLCH MARTIX—8 *
(NMPSLLCH PAR—9
(NPPALLCH PIOR—10
(NPPCLLCH QUALQUER—11
(NMPSLLCH DOR—12
(NMPCLLCH POR—13
(NPPSLLCH MULHER—14
(NPPSLLCH LUGAR—15
(NPPSLLCH COMPUTADOR—16
(NPPSLLCH PESQUISADOR—17
(NMPSLLCH AR—18
(NPPSLLCH CANCER—19

Appendix 7.12. Informant F codification

F = ESTAURINA – 46 – LOWER CLASS – (46-60)

Informal Interview

(NPCAILCF MAIOR—1
(NPCAILCF PIOR—2
(NMVSILCF BAR—3
(NMVSILCF COR—4
(DPCSILCF INTERIOX—5 *
(NMVSILCF LAR—6
(NPCSILCF PARTICULAR—7
(DPCAILCF MELHOX—8 *
(DPVSILCF COMPUTADOX—9 *
(DPCSILCF VENDEDOX—10 *
(NPPSILCF JUNIOR—11
(NPCSILCF COMPRADOR—12

Text

(NPCSTLCF FAVOR—1
(NPVSTLCF AMOR—2
(DPPCTLCF QUALQUEX—3 *
(NPVATLCF MAIOR—4
(NPCSTLCF HORROR—5
(NMVSTLCF DOR—6
(NPCATLCF SUPER—7
(NPCSTLCF POPULAR—8
(NPPSTLCF SONHADOR—9
(NPCSTLCF INTERIOR—10
(NPPSTLCF IMPERADOR—11
(NPCSTLCF FAVOR—12
(NPVSTLCF AMOR—13
(NPCSTLCF LIDER—14
(NPCSTLCF MARTIR—15
(NPPATLCF POPULAR—16
(NPCSTLCF TREINADOR—17

(NPVSTLCF AMOR—18
(NMCCTLCF POR—19
(NPVSTLCF PRAZER—20
(NMPSTLCF LAR—21
(NPVSTLCF TRABALHADOR—22
(NMCSTLCF FLOR—23
(NPCSTLCF PRAZER—24
(NPCSTLCF TELESPECTADOR—25
(NPPSTLCF NARRADOR—26

Word List

(NPPALLCF MAIOR—1
(NPPSLLCF ABAJUR—2
(NMPSLLCF MAR—3
(NPPALLCF SUPER—4
(NPPSLLCF FEMUR—5
(NPPSLLCF SONHADOR—6
(NPPALLCF MENOR—7
(NPPSLLCF MARTIR—8
(NMPSLLCF PAR—9
(NPPALLCF PIOR—10
(NPPCLLCF QUALQUER—11
(NMPSLLCF DOR—12
(NMPCLLCF POR—13
(NPPSLLCF MULHER—14
(NPPSLLCF LUGAR—15
(NPPSLLCF COMPUTADOR—16
(NPPSLLCF PESQUISADOR—17
(NMPSLLCF AR—18
(NPPSLLCF CANCER—19

Printed in the United States
By Bookmasters